Contents

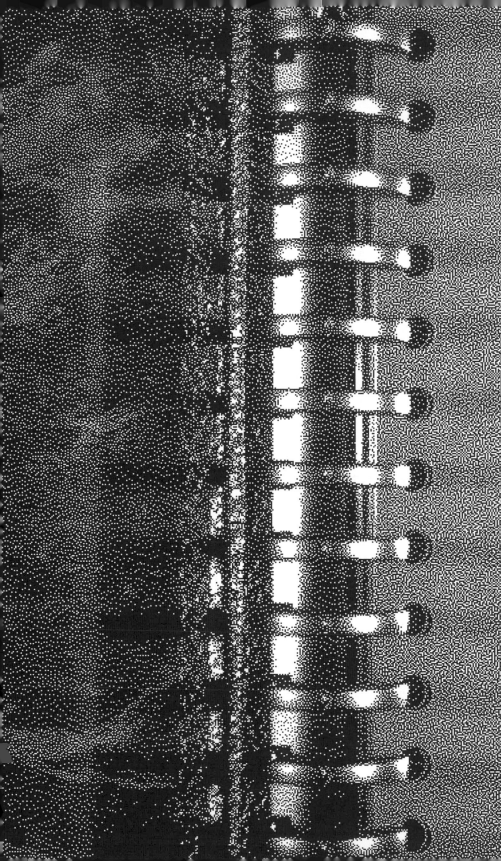

How to Prepare Your Portfolio

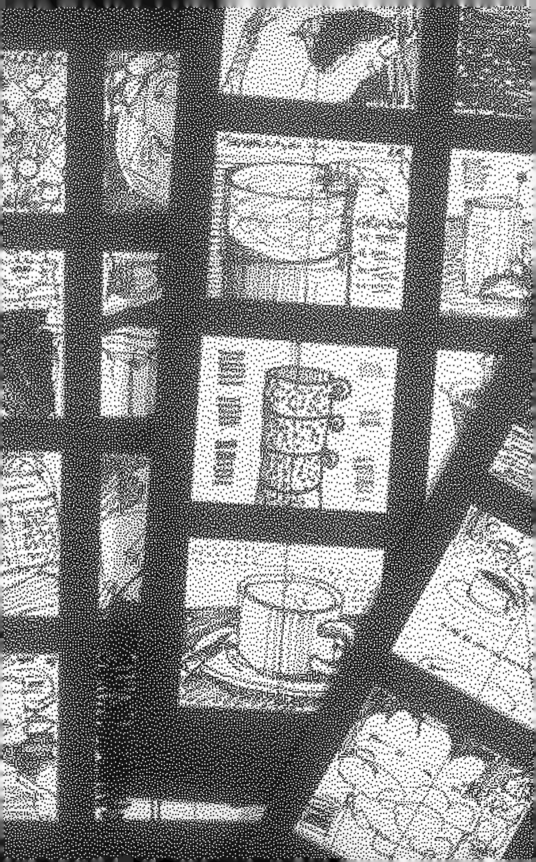

How to Prepare Your Portfolio

A Guide for Students and Professionals

Ed Marquand

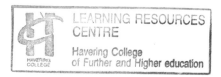
Art Direction Book Company, Inc.

The author would like to thank members of his staff
for their assistance in preparing this revised edition.
Special thanks to John Hubbard and Marie Weiler, as
well as Audrey Jawando, Cynthia McBride, and Pamela
Zytnicki. Thanks also to the designers who allowed
me to photograph their portfolio pieces, including
Jo David, Bret Granato, Vikki Leib, Tiffany Linnes,
and Bruce Pritchard.

Twentieth Century Plastics in Brea, California,
was generous in allowing me to photograph many of
their fine portfolio products for this book.

I am also grateful to my patient, yet persistent,
publisher, Don Barron.

Third edition, revised, 1994
Second Printing 1999
Copyright © 1981 Ed Marquand

LCC# 81-66881
ISBN 0-88108-144-2 cloth
ISBN 0-88108-143-4 paper

Edited by Marie Weiler
Printed in the United States of America

Published by
Art Direction Book Company, Inc.
456 Glenbrook Rd.
Glenbrook, CT 06906

Introduction

The staggering numbers of art- and design-school graduates that enter the professional world each year make for extremely competitive job markets in both of these fields. Historically, many parents have discouraged their children from art and design careers, often because of the lack of job security those professions provide. Now, even art and design professors are offering the same warnings. It *is* tough out there, but you will eventually find success if you take to heart a few pieces of simple advice: be resourceful, be constantly on the lookout for opportunities, become more than just competent in your profession, and be persistent. Remember, there is always room for the best in any profession.

If you are like most beginning designers and artists, you are scrambling to put together a portfolio to show prospective employers. But, in that classic vicious cycle, you don't have many pieces to show because you've never had a job, and you can't get a job without impressive pieces in your portfolio. Or, you have a job, but it isn't as creative as you'd like, so you try to find another one but you don't have extraordinary examples because your current job isn't very creative. . . . And so on. The best way to break this cycle is to create examples for your portfolio that are up to the level you are trying to achieve. One of the themes of this book is the importance of investing the time to create stronger work specifically for your portfolio. Remember, an investment in your portfolio is an investment in your future; you will be refining your skills at the same time you create the pieces to make yourself more salable.

Chapter 1

Nine Steps to a Professional Portfolio

Approach the preparation of your portfolio in a logical and organized manner. The following steps should prompt you to face the major content issues first, followed by details of reproduction, construction, and assembly.

Step 1 Determine what you want your portfolio to do for you and what kind of portfolio you need.

Step 2 Determine what type of artist or designer you are and where you are likely to find your best opportunities.

Step 3 Compile, edit, and select your artwork.

Step 4 Select a binder and format for your portfolio.

Step 5 Organize your work graphically or thematically.

Step 6 Convert your artwork to a size that will fit your portfolio format.

Step 7 Assemble all the pieces.

Step 8 Review your résumé or leave-behinds.

Step 9 Keep samples, and document your work.

Step 1

Determine what you want your portfolio to do for you.

Are you looking for a job? Full time or part-time fill-in? Are you looking for freelance work that might lead to a regular job? Are you looking strictly for assignment work? Do you want someone to act as your agent and represent your work? Are you trying to find entry-level work, or do you want to come across as a seasoned professional?

Three types of professional portfolios can help you achieve the look you require:

- the job hunter's portfolio
- the freelancer's portfolio
- the fine artist's or illustrator's portfolio.

Although you can sometimes get by with a more general one, you're usually better off if you tailor your portfolio to specific goals, so let's look at each one in turn.

The Job Hunter's Portfolio

If you're looking for a staff position in a design studio or art department, your portfolio is one of the major points your potential employer will consider when evaluating you as a future employee. Unless you are applying for a job that entails specialized work, you should include samples that show a broad range of abilities and experience. You should give the impression that you can solve any problem your employer hands you, that you are talented, resourceful, and professional.

Your book can show skill and experience, but it can also reinforce other qualities such as consistency and attention to detail. Your interviewer will be looking for tip-offs to your work habits and personal style. Just as misspelled words on your résumé count against you, so too do sloppy mounting, dog-eared corners, and poorly reproduced artwork. When competition is tough and quality of artwork is about even, the designer who comes across as the most thorough will have the best chance of being hired.

The Freelancer's Portfolio

As a freelancer, you, and your portfolio, are judged differently. Since you will not be a staff member, rather than demonstrate your ability to fit into the studio's routine, you want to demonstrate solid professional experience in the specific skills for which you are being considered. Your portfolio should concentrate on well-aimed, high-quality examples and less on general abilities. Of course, if the freelance work has the potential of becoming a staff position, the same points raised in the job hunter's portfolio apply here.

The Fine Artist's or Illustrator's Portfolio

If you are a fine artist or illustrator, you may need to circulate your work among galleries or artist agents to be considered for representation. Your portfolio should include only reproductions of finished, fully developed pieces of art, usually in slide, transparency, or color-print form. It is more important to show your work clearly and accurately than to show mechanical or technical abilities. Printed examples of your work from magazines or catalogues can be included as support, but concentrate on the art first, featuring it to its best and clearest advantage.

Determining what you want your portfolio to do for you is the first step in its planning. However, if you want full-time work and jobs are scarce, freelance work might be a good way to get your foot in the door. Also, consult friends or colleagues in the profession; they might have suggestions for ways to approach your search. Time spent researching your professional opportunities before you prepare your portfolio will give you more confidence as you edit the material you are considering for inclusion. As much as possible, try to determine where you fit within your profession and build your portfolio accordingly.

Step 2

Determine what type of artist or designer you are and where you are likely to find your best opportunities.
If you are looking for work, you may not have time for much self-examination, but a clear-headed look at your talents, skills, experience, and ambitions is a useful exercise as you start to prepare your portfolio. The better you understand yourself, and your relation to your

profession, the better you will be able to decide how to present yourself in interviews and in your portfolio. You should also take stock of the areas of your profession that are most likely to present opportunities. You need to be secure in your abilities, but you will also have to find potential employers who have needs to be met and problems to be solved. Let's discuss evaluating your work first.

Most designers or artists who have made it through school or worked in a design job know what they can do well, with speed, accuracy, and grace. They also know the techniques that come less easily and tasks they should avoid all together. It's wonderful, though rare, for a novice to find a position ideally suited to his or her gifts; dues usually have to be paid. Frustrating and sometimes menial tasks are part of all professions, and design and art production has its share.

Most job seekers and freelancers wonder, What can I do well enough to make me immediately employable? Identify your skills. Play them up and show them off. They are your strongest assets, and you should build your portfolio around them. If necessary, create new artwork to demonstrate talents not otherwise illustrated. On the other hand, if you know you will never excel in certain skills, don't try to fake it, as it might bring down the overall quality of your portfolio. Spend your time on the work that has the most potential to impress prospective employers.

Aside from individual talents, it is good to know whether you are more of a generalist or a specialist. If you perform many kinds of tasks well, pick up new skills quickly, and enjoy learning new approaches and techniques, you are probably better suited to a job that allows you to solve many different kinds of problems and gives you a range of responsibilities. Select work for your portfolio that reflects this tendency, and discuss it at your interviews. On the other hand, if you like perfecting one thing at a time, perhaps to the point of obsession, you are a specialist and should look for opportunities where that trait will be appreciated.

This self-knowledge is good to have, but until you can display it to a potential employer its value is limited. The most successful design and art professionals are constantly looking for opportunities and understand that often the best jobs and assignments are awarded through personal contacts. If a design firm has an opening and the employer is personally acquainted with someone qualified for the job, he or she might forgo the time and expense of advertising and interviewing. For that reason, it is immensely important to maintain a network of friends already working in the profession. The opportunity to help out during a particularly busy time can open the door to a permanent position. Work study and apprenticeships can provide excellent professional experience, references, and contacts—compensation for the low wages these positions usually pay.

The longer one remains in a profession, the easier the networking process becomes, but for those new to the field, it can be difficult to develop this skill. The best way to start is to get to know as many professionals in your areas of interest as possible. Your friends from school, instructors, counselors, and any professionals you know personally will form the basis for your network, and professional organizations and activities will increase your opportunities for meeting new colleagues. Attend and participate in professional workshops and lectures to help familiarize yourself with the issues, concerns, and players active in your specialty. This will increase your exposure, allowing others to get to know you. And, since this factor is so important, remember that clients and employers like to work with artists and designers they know and enjoy. Social skills do count; if yours need work, work on them.

It is also essential for you to understand your role from your potential employer's perspective. As an employee or freelance artist, your primary function will be to help your employer realize a profit by saving time and energy and by honoring the studio's professional commitments. Keep this uppermost in your mind when you are thinking of ways to get work. Remember that it is not the employer's immediate concern how the work you may be hired to do fits into your career path or vision of success, or whether the work you are expected to do is "beneath" you or too unsophisticated. A professional designer learns early that if the work is good enough to take on, it is worthy of the designer's best efforts. Don't underestimate the importance of showing or telling your interviewer that you are a good worker, willing to put in extra time and effort to do a job right. Though this may seem like a small point, it is remarkable how few job applicants make this specific point clear.

With all of this self-awareness and professional perspective you can move on to the next step of planning your portfolio.

Step 3

Compile, edit, and select your artwork.
If you have kept your best pieces or have taken good photographs of them, this step will be a simple matter of picking and choosing, but if you haven't, you will have a more difficult time. It is important to document your best work, either in photographs or in printed samples. Your experience is difficult to demonstrate if you don't have the evidence. (See the section on keeping samples and documenting your work at the end of this chapter.)

Once you have gathered all your work, compare and evaluate it. Establish criteria and test each piece against those standards. Is the piece a good example? Does it reinforce the points you want your portfolio to make? Is it work you are proud of? Would another piece make the same points more clearly? Is the piece contemporary? Are there simple repairs or corrections you could make that would improve the piece? Does this collection of samples represent the primary skills you are trying to demonstrate? Are your selections redundant?

If you have too many pieces that have survived this critical examination, leave them in for now. Some will reproduce better than others, and you can decide later which will be the most effective in your book. If you don't have enough, consider how you can fill in the gaps, but never include clearly inferior work just to have something to show. Inferior pieces drag down the quality of the best pieces, and call your judgment into question. When in doubt, leave it out—unless you know you are being unreasonable, and then ask a trusted friend or adviser to tell you the truth. Nearly every art director who reviews portfolios will tell you that most novices include too much mediocre work; they could strengthen their cases with judicial editing.

Select a binder and format for your portfolio.

Step 4

Now that you know what you are going to put into your portfolio, you can think about the kind of presentation you want to make. At the end of Chapter 3, we will review a variety of styles and their accessories. Meanwhile, here are some questions to consider as you think about what best suits your style.

Multi-ring binders are sturdy and practical. This style might be best if you need to present your work in a particular sequence or if you are concerned about keeping pieces of artwork together.

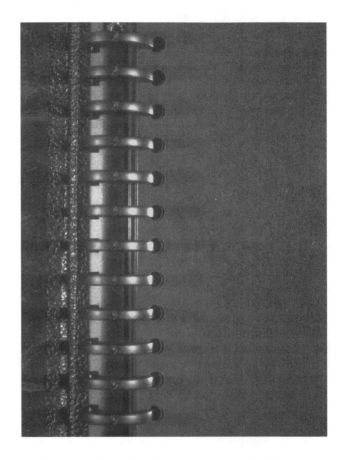

- Will you be showing your portfolio in person, or is it likely that you will have to leave it for someone to review?
- Will you be mailing your portfolio?
- Will you be carrying your portfolio long distances? on subways? airplanes?
- Is most of your original artwork large or small?
- Will you need to change your presentation before every appointment?

- Will you need more than one copy of the portfolio?
- Will you be presenting your portfolio frequently, or just until you land a job?

Consider carefully the choice of binder or carrying case. There are many different kinds on the market today, some very attractive and functional. Your case will determine much about the look, heft, durability, and design of your portfolio. Here are some points to consider.

Size: Portfolio cases range from small to large, but you will find the best selection in small to medium sizes. If all your work needs to be shown in slide sheets or transparency holders, a three-ring binder might make the most sense. They are light, easy to carry and duplicate, and can be mailed for a reasonable cost. In addition, there are many styles of binder covers, and plastic protectors and slide pages are readily available for this format.

In most cases, it is better to have large design work or illustrations reduced to fit your portfolio than to drag it around to interviews, exposing it to unnecessary wear. In tight quarters, oversize work can be difficult to present because of the table space it requires. And if you will be traveling with the work you should consider whether you would be willing to check it as baggage with an airline. If you decide you must have a large portfolio, select a carrying case rather than a large ring binder. That way

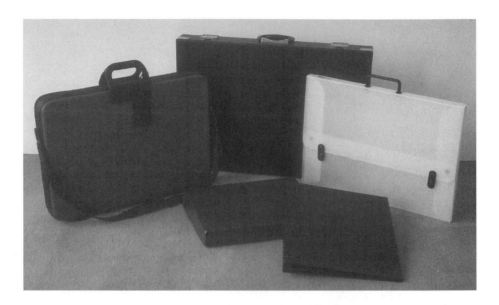

if your interviewer is pressed for table space, you can pull out one piece at a time.

Medium-size cases are usually the most suitable for design work, photography, and illustrations.

Style: The most popular portfolio cases have multi-ring binding and come with plastic protector pages. You can get similar carrying cases without the rings. If you want to keep your work in a sequence and if your presentations will be similar, a multi-ring binder makes sense. This style works well when you must leave your portfolio for review at a design firm.

Designers who require more flexibility and will always be presenting their work in person, may prefer a storyboard. In this style each item is loose, sometimes mounted onto a piece of board or laminated. This format allows you to tailor your presentation to the occasion, adding or removing items at any time and even passing over some samples in the interview, if time, or the interviewer's interest, is running short .

Durability: Pick a case and protector pages that will hold up over time and will withstand many presentations. This is particularly important if you are looking for freelance work. Your portfolio case, sleeves, backings, and storyboard mounts should be maintained and replaced as they show signs of wear.

Orientation: If most of your work is horizontal, design your layouts accordingly. Keep your mounts as consistent in size as possible.

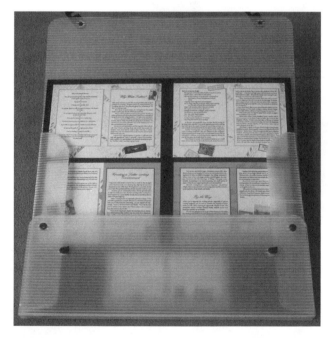

If you need an inexpensive carrying case, this model works well. These presentation boards were designed and cut to fit this portfolio case.

Step 5

Organize your work graphically or thematically.

Throughout the process of selecting and editing your work, be thinking of how to best organize it. Depending on how you plan to show your work, you may want to start out with an overview of your experience and then return to a few specific projects in more depth. Or you may want to start with your strongest seven or eight pieces, hit hard with them, and then sup-

This designer has laminated all of her printed samples and presents her work one piece at a time. She can easily tailor her portfolio presentation to each interview.

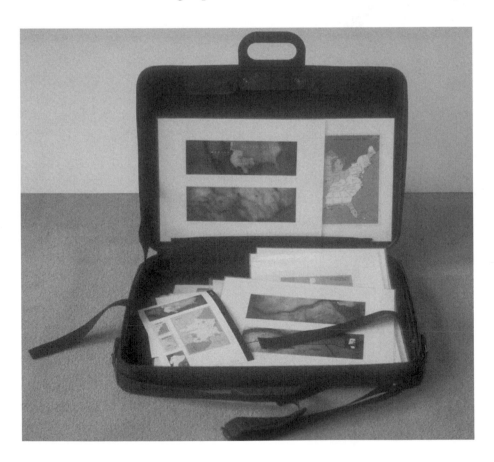

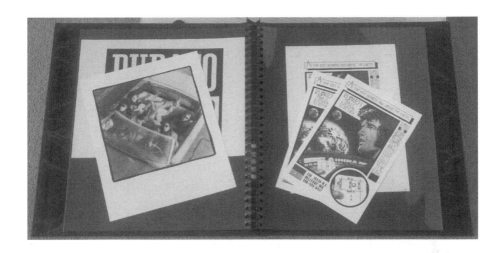

port them with less impressive, but technically proficient, examples. Try rehearsing typical interview situations to come up with a good organizational scheme. If you discover that your presentation isn't working the way you planned, tailor the organization to make it flow more naturally.

This designer includes loose art, photographs, and extras of printed pieces in his multi-ring binder. He can easily slip them out to show in an interview.

Convert your artwork to size.

Most artists and designers will have to reproduce their artwork to get it to fit the design and layout of their portfolio. You may be able to do this with photocopies, or you may have to hire a professional photographer to shoot your examples. There are many processes and techniques available to you. They are discussed in greater detail in Chapters 3 and 7.

Step 6

Assemble your portfolio.

With your binder selected, your artwork photographed, and your supplies in hand, you can

Step 7

begin to put your portfolio together. In Chapter 4 we will review techniques for mounting and displaying artwork in a portfolio.

Step 8

Review your résumé or leave-behinds.

Support your portfolio with a solid résumé. Review all of the information you plan to include, then proofread for spelling, punctuation, and grammar. Make sure your design is clear, concise, and professional. Run off enough copies to get you through many interviews: as your primary leave-behind, you will want to be able to hand it out freely.

Finished printed pieces for a single client may be organized in project folders and included within a larger portfolio.

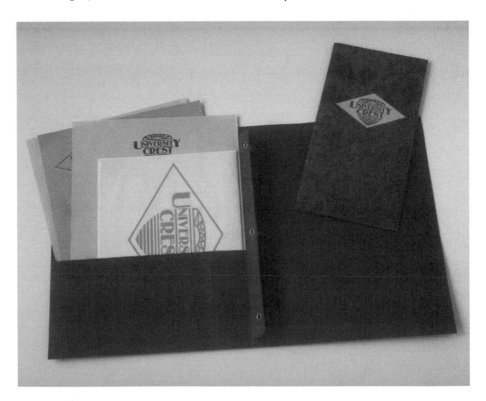

In Chapter 5 we will review some suggestions for improving your résumé. There are also several good books on effective résumé preparation.

Keep samples, and document your work. Step 9

To keep your portfolio up to date, make a habit of collecting samples of your work or photographing originals as soon as you finish them.

If you are a graphic designer or production artist, ask your employer or client—before the work is sent to the printer—to set aside several samples of the finished product. Better still, ask about receiving samples when you begin work on the project, so the client understands how

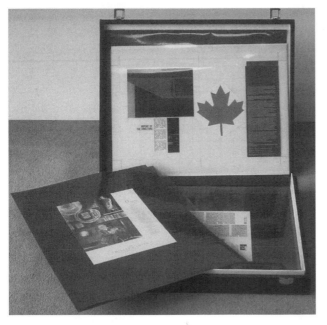

This designer's portfolio is a series of presentation boards of assignments. The boards are all a uniform size. He stores his best artwork in sturdy cases to keep them fresh and in good condition.

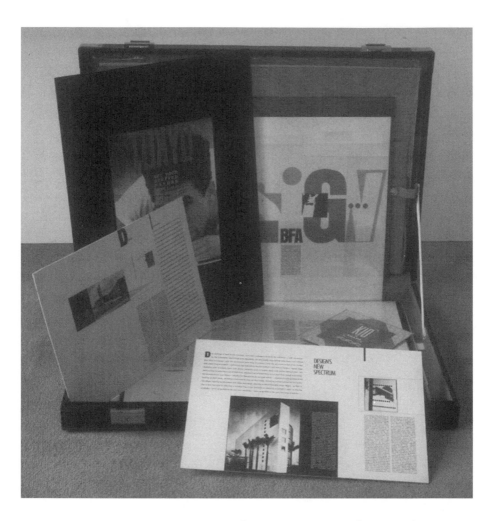

You can also keep design boards of various sizes in portfolio cases, presenting only the appropriate pieces during each interview.

important they are to you and can make arrangements for printing enough copies. Make your request specific, and be sure to ask that the samples be given to you as soon as they are delivered from the printer, or they may all be distributed or sent to the client. Be persistent; these samples are important assets for your future. If there aren't enough samples for your client to spare any, ask if you can borrow one to photograph or photocopy.

If you are a fine artist or illustrator who sells the originals, photograph your work regularly. Your work will look its best immediately after you finish it, while colors are fresh and the work is clean. If you can't do it yourself, have it done professionally. Most art schools, art departments, or art supply stores post ads or notices on bulletin boards advertising for this service. Professional photo labs and art galleries are usually good sources for leads on this kind of photography.

Interior designers and architects face additional problems. They lose possession of most of their finished products, be they interiors, finished homes, displays, or commercial projects, so it becomes even more important to photograph the work as soon as it is complete.

Those are the steps you will go through to prepare a professional portfolio. In the following chapters we will discuss the specific approaches for several kinds of designers' portfolios, and the mechanics of assembly.

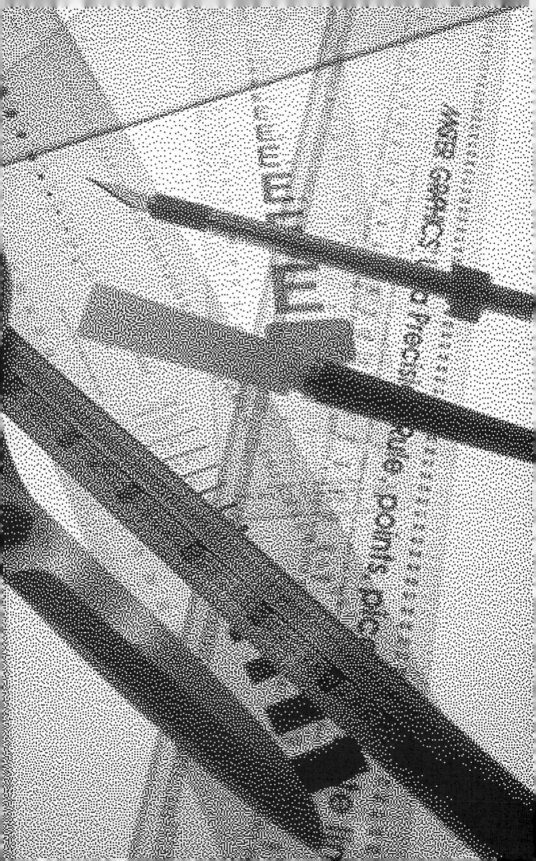

Chapter 2

Examples of Professional Portfolios

To give you some ideas of ways to organize and display your work, we will discuss how a number of design professionals might approach the problem. Don't limit yourself to these examples. Apply your own imagination to this design problem.

Graphic Designer's Portfolio

Whether you are looking for a full-time job or freelance work you will want to show your experience solving a variety of design problems, familiarity with production details and techniques, computer experience, printing, sensitivity to typography, and art direction experience. The computer has become so central to graphic design that it is important that you demonstrate mastery of the basic software programs as well. If you are just entering the job market, you may demonstrate all of these skills by creating pieces for your portfolio with computer-generated artwork.

Design schools encourage students to assemble full-blown design projects such as imaginary annual reports, complex booklets, or posters on famous designers. But if you are looking for your first design job, the work you will be hired to do immediately is more likely to be the quick one-color ad or flier. Show

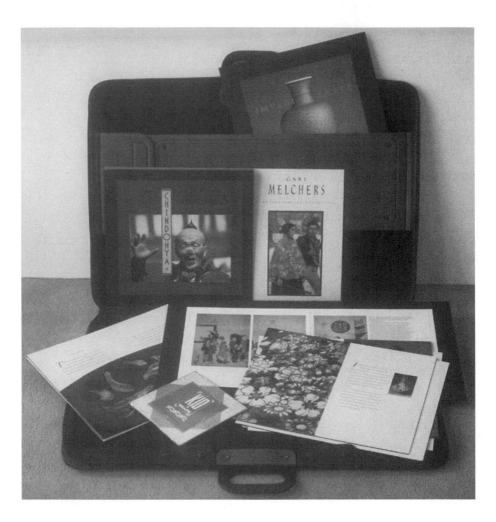

This designer keeps his best presentation boards for past projects and can show interviewers several optional designs for projects, not just the ones that were selected.

how much imagination you can bring to this kind of design problem, and you will probably come closer to your potential employer's immediate needs.

To show how you have solved art direction or design problems, you could create binder pages or presentation boards describing and illustrating the problems, paired with their solutions. "Before-and-afters" can be impressive, so don't be afraid to put several in your portfolio. If you are new to the job market and don't have many samples to show, create design problems for yourself from existing materials in sore need of design help, and develop some of your own before-and-afters. In this same vein, showing a brochure from a quickly sketched concept, to handmade rough dummy, to tight comp, to printed piece could demonstrate your skills at the major design stages.

Finished printed pieces demonstrate real production experience best, but it isn't difficult to generate some good examples of mechanical production using a computer and service-bureau output. The days of showing samples of paste-up work are over.

This designer keeps comps and printed samples in clamshell-style archival boxes. He has several magazines, menus, brochures, and before-and-afters.

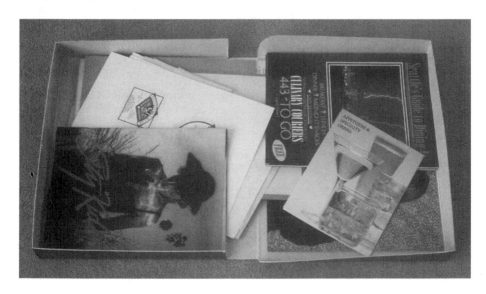

Here, the designer has decided to show a rough with the final printed piece. This reveals your working style and quick-comping skills to an interviewer.

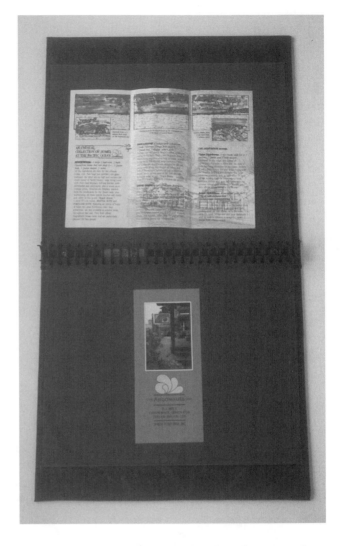

Typography, on the other hand, is a craft that will never become obsolete, and with all the fonts and publishing programs so readily available on computers, your typography examples should go well beyond the lettering exercises of a decade ago.

Sketching and storyboard drawing are always impressive. A frequent comment by art directors is that recent design graduates do so much work on computer that they no longer have the traditional hand skills, so this might be one way to distinguish your work.

Production Artist's Portfolio

If you are looking for graphic design production work but are not interested in design work, make this clear in your résumé and portfolio. Stress it in your interviews by including challenging pieces that you did not design. This way, you can get credit for doing difficult and impressive production work, whether or not the design is successful. Until recently, you could include sample mechanicals with overlays, Rubyliths, and keylines, but since they

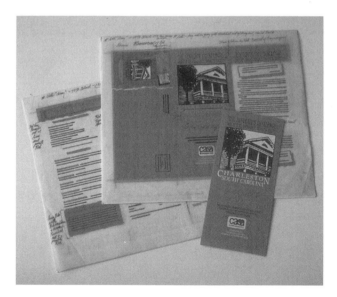

A production artist who can give clear instructions to a printer is smart to show this skill by including mechanicals and final pieces in the portfolio.

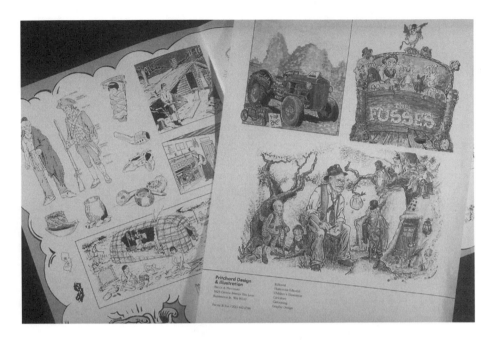

Bruce Pritchard shows his work with the help of four-color fliers featuring recent examples of his illustration and cartooning. He sends these to ad agencies, art directors, designers, and other potential clients.

are quickly becoming things of the past, think about samples you can include that show off your ability to do complex production on the computer.

Beautifully done map production, either traditionally produced or computer generated, is impressive, especially when it shows evidence of clean, tight, and obsessively neat habits.

Illustrator's Portfolio

As an illustrator you are probably looking for assignment work rather than a staff position. If you are extremely versatile in style and medium, show that range. If your style is more focused and individual, show how you apply it to a variety of assignments.

Though finished pieces show real professional experience, original artwork shows what you can do. Progressive stages can show an art director how you work and your ability to adjust or modify an illustration. Rough sketches, tighter comps, and the finished piece can make a strong case for your work. Art directors like to work with illustrators who can accommodate their direction and revisions.

Even if your preferred style is complex and highly evolved, include some basic, simpler work among your examples. If they are good, they might get you some work. Basic line drawing and cartooning have broad application and are used more frequently than fully rendered illustrations. If you can demonstrate the basics and give them your own twist of style, you will find more work for yourself.

Photographer's Portfolio

As a photographer, preparing your portfolio should be a simple matter of selecting your images, enlarging the prints, mounting the transparencies, and assembling them into your book. If you have printed samples from magazines, newspapers, brochures, or books, include them with your originals. (Since most photos suffer in reproduction, show your interviewer the quality of your originals.)

If you shoot 4 × 5" or 8 × 10" transparencies, mount them in holders instead of showing them as prints. It's unlikely that you will get the same intense, clear colors from a print.

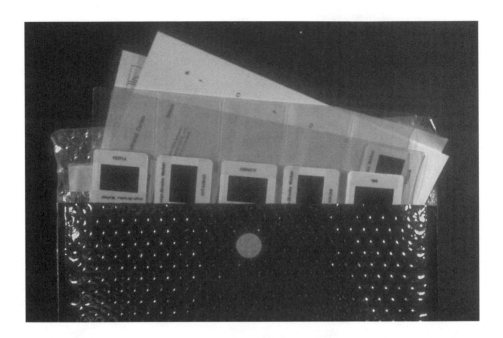

This photographer's portfolio couldn't be simpler. A letter, résumé, and slides pages have been packaged in a bubble-wrap envelope.

If you shoot in the smaller formats—35mm or 2¼"—and if you plan to show your work to art directors and designers who are used to viewing them, you can mount and show your original film with a loupe. But if your clients will find prints easier to inspect, show enlargements instead. When you show prints, they should be flawlessly printed and properly mounted.

The images you select for your portfolio should reflect your professional ambitions. As with all the visual and graphic professions, photography has become highly specialized. Advertising photography is much different than studio portraiture. Architectural photography is a world away from fashion or photojournalism. If you have a specialty, play it up. On the other hand, if you want to be considered for a variety of assignments, select images accordingly.

Your specialty might affect the form of your originals. Ad agencies reviewing "table top" or studio shots will expect to see highly refined, large format transparencies. Portrait studios will want to see examples of color and black-and-white prints. Newspapers will usually accept 35mm slides and, of course, black-and-white prints.

Architect's and Interior Designer's Portfolio

Here, it is important to distinguish students from practicing professionals. Let's start with recent graduates looking for jobs in design firms.

For most architects and designers beginning professional careers, demonstration of the basic skills is more important than a con-

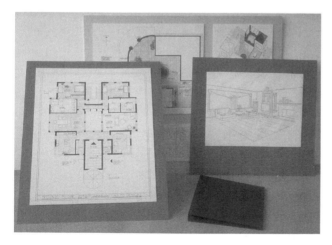

Architects and interior designers have to find the best way to show large renderings, drawings, and blueprints. This designer has mounted only her best work; the bulk of it she has reduced, for display in her portfolio binder.

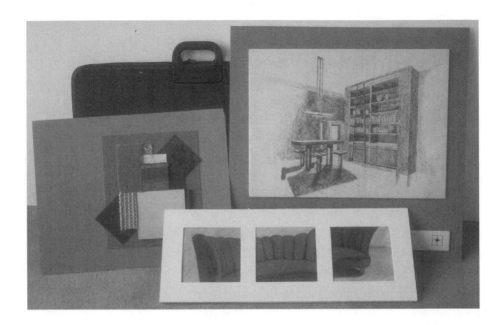

Unfortunately for interior designers, there is no easy way to show sample boards. A good solution is to make fewer boards, each one so good that it conveys the quality and expertise of wider experience, and to carry photographs of all of the others you want to show.

centration on design. Show design, of course, but feature the skills you will need to use immediately in your new job. Show course work, thesis projects, and assignments, but redo them, or several of them, taking advantage of the lessons you learned the first time around. Modify the subjects or approaches so they aren't exactly like your first efforts. Prove to your interviewer that you are a step or two beyond your classmates and that you are willing to work harder to demonstrate your talents. You will probably discover that your redone pieces are better than your assignment work. They will certainly be neater, cleaner, and fresher looking, and you may be surprised how much further you can push some of your best ideas.

Accomplished architects and designers need to show completed projects, or at least finished plans, when they change jobs. Photographs of existing buildings or interiors are important. Plans and documentation will support your claims, and published work is especially impressive.

Fine Artist's Portfolio

For a fine artist who is showing work to galleries, museums, art consultants, or competition judges, a good portfolio can be as simple as a selection of transparencies and slides, carefully labeled and organized, supported by published reviews, catalogues, and articles featuring your work and followed by a biography and bibliography. In the art marketplace, slides and transparencies are the most common form for presenting artwork. The assumption is that most original artwork is too large or too delicate to take around. Typically, galleries screen work by reviewing photographs first, and see the original work later if they are interested.

As easy as it is to organize a fine artist's portfolio, good photography is a must. A large painting will lose a lot as a 35mm slide but can look dazzling as a 4 × 5" or 8 × 10" transparency. High-quality transparencies, however, require the services of a professional photographer. Take the time to shop around for a good studio. Art galleries may be able to provide names of photographers who specialize in this work.

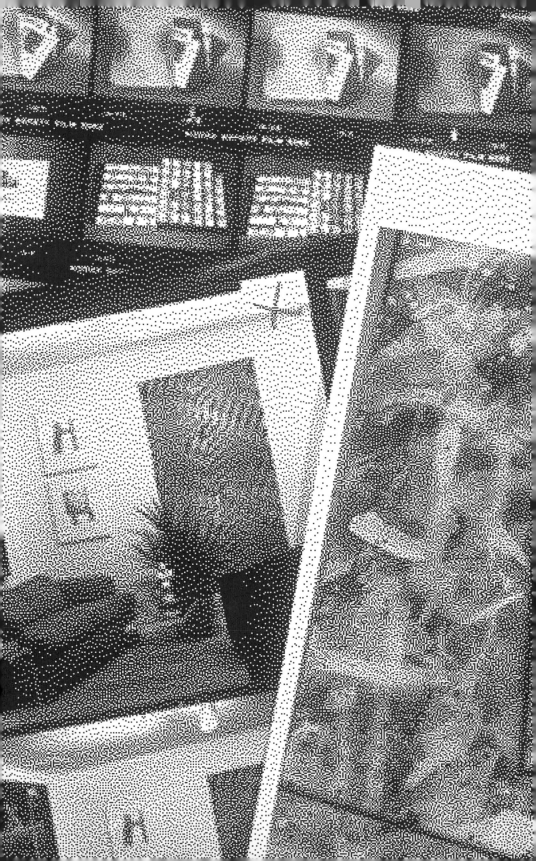

Chapter 3

Fitting Your Work to the Portfolio Format

In the last chapter we discussed what to include in your portfolio. In this chapter we will investigate the various processes available to reproduce your work to display size. Then we will demonstrate ways to mount and display different kinds of work in binders with binder accessories.

Methods for Reproducing Your Work

To keep things simple, we will classify the reproduction processes into three categories: photo, graphic, and computer generated. Although there is some overlap between them, the distinctions are useful. Basically, photo processes are those that require a camera and film. Slides and transparencies and color and black-and-white paper enlargements fall into this group. Graphic processes include stats and transfers and color and black-and-white photocopying. Computer-generated processes include typesetting, service-bureau output, and laser printouts.

The Photo Processes

If you need to photograph your artwork or if you are a photographer, you will work with one or more of the following processes.

35mm transparencies: Commonly referred to as color slides, these are a direct process, meaning that, once it has been processed, the film you put in your camera becomes the original. Slides do not need to be converted from negatives to positives.

Color transparencies: These are similar to slides except in size, which ranges from 2¼" square to 8 × 10". Four-by-five inch transparencies are the standard in many professions. When properly shot, they have excellent color saturation and detail. For high-quality printing most color separators prefer to reproduce from 4 × 5" or 8 × 10" original transparencies.

Color or black-and-white negatives: If your photographs will need to be printed as enlargements, you can achieve the best quality by shooting negative film and having enlargements made from the negatives. Color prints made from color negatives are generally better quality than prints made from transparencies, because negatives give the darkroom technician greater control over the color adjustment and saturation. It is possible, however, for a skilled technician to make excellent color prints from good quality slides and transparencies.

When professionals shoot negatives they develop the film as contact sheets, which are small positives of each image. From this, the photographer can select the individual exposures to print as enlargements.

Color or black-and-white enlargements:
When you want to reproduce your image from film to paper, you have your negative enlarged. For best results, have your processing and printing done at a professional photo lab.

Black-and-white prints are usually printed on resin-coated paper. If you need something richer, more like fine art or portrait photographs, you will need to specify that they be printed on fiber-based paper. Fiber-based prints are more expensive and are usually available only at professional labs. If you are not sure of the distinctions between the two kinds of prints, ask someone at the photo lab to show you examples of each.

Color prints: Here you are faced with a couple of choices, but the basic process is the same and the differences are mostly those of quality.

C-prints are made from your negatives, which are enlarged to the proper size and printed. Depending on the skill of the printer and the quality of your original negative, it is possible to get excellent color saturation and detail with C-prints. Professional labs offer several degrees of quality, charging extra to manipulate your negative in order to bring out the qualities you are trying to achieve. Sizes for C-prints usually run from 8 × 10" to a maximum of 20 × 24", the largest being quite expensive.

R-prints are made directly from transparencies, without using a negative. With this positive-to-positive process, the printer has some control over exposure, but color correction is much more difficult than with C-prints.

Cibachrome enlargements are high-contrast prints made from transparencies, using various materials and techniques. They have highly saturated color and a high-gloss finish, best suited to high-contrast and dramatic photographs.

Dye-transfer is another color-print process popular with fine arts photographers. It is a laborious process, not usually suited for general portfolio work.

Before placing your order, ask the photo lab how much they will charge for the work you require; you might want to discuss alternate processes that give comparable quality but are less expensive. Also, find out how much time the lab needs to do the work without charging rush fees, which can run as high as 100 percent for quick turnaround work.

Laser color: In the past few years the improvements in color photocopying have been dramatic. Not only has quality improved, but availability and affordablity have improved as well. For many artists and designers who can't afford professional quality enlargements for their portfolios, laser copies might be the best alternative. Most machines can enlarge images up to 11 × 17".

Color laser prints can be made from positive originals small enough to fit on an 11 × 17" copyboard or from slides and transparencies.

Slides are projected onto the copyboard, while transparencies have light projected through the image in direct contact with the copyboard. As a rule, paper positive originals copy better than slides or transparencies, and bold, graphic work reproduces better than delicate, subtle work. But trying different exposures and different machines can net dramatically different results. You are limited to the amount of reduction or enlargement the machine can produce in a single exposure, since copies of copies degrade. For many applications, however, laser copies are the best way to go. Photocopy machines vary in quality, consistency, and price, so you may want to shop around to find the best resource for your needs.

The Graphic Processes

If you want to include type, line illustrations, maps, diagrams, or charts in your portfolio, you will need to use one of the graphic processes described in this section. Most of these processes were developed for advertising and graphics studios to help create comprehensive layouts and design presentations. These "comps" could be used to show clients what an ad or design would look like in its final form before going to the effort and expense of producing the actual item. For many designers these techniques and processes will be useful for preparing examples of design work for their portfolios, especially if they don't have actual printed samples.

Until recently, photostats and the related photomechanical processes were commonly used, but the overwhelming popularity and flexibility of computer programs and output devices have caused the traditional techniques to fall by the wayside. If, however, you do not work with a computer, the traditional methods work just fine. We will briefly review the traditional media, and then discuss the more common photocopying methods.

Photostats: For several decades, if you designed a logo, created a piece of line art, or drew a finely lined illustration, you produced your work by hand and then reproduced it to various sizes by means of photostats—high-contrast black-and-white photographs.

If you have any of the types of artwork described above, contact graphic- and art-supply stores to see if they can recommend a local vendor. Determine from the descriptions below what type of stat or stats you need, then size your artwork before you send it off to have your positive prints, film overlays, halftone prints, or color transfers made.

- **Positive prints:** Let's say you have a series of line drawings that you want to include in your portfolio as high-quality, high-contrast black-and-white prints. First, determine how large you want them. Then decide how much of a plain border you need around each image. Next, size each image to the percentage of the original you want it to be. For example, if you want to

reduce a 10" drawing to 5", you will need a
50-percent stat. If you have a 7" print you
want reproduced to 14", you will need a
200-percent stat. Finally, be sure to clean
up any dirt or lines you do not want reproduced.

- **Halftone prints:** If your image has tone
  and you want to show that tone, you will
  need a halftone stat. This is slightly more
  expensive than a line stat. If you have a
  wash drawing and you would like the sur-
  rounding paper to come out pure white,
  you will need to ask the stat supplier for a
  drop-out halftone. In this type of halftone,
  the original is shot with a contrast range
  that eliminates any black dots from pure
  white areas.
- **Transfer processes:** Many photostat ven-
  dors also provide transfer services. Say, for
  example, you want to have colored type on
  a colored paper background and drawing
  the type will not give you the high quality

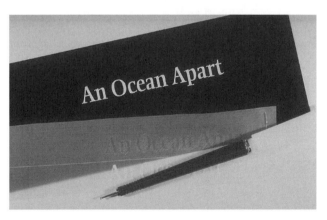

Custom rubdown type
can be used to create
color effects for design
pieces.

Like rubdown transfer processes, photocopy coloring techniques approximate printed color.

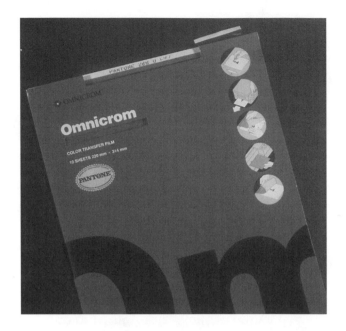

you are looking for. You can either have color transfers made that are screen printed directly onto colored paper, or you can have rubdowns made in the color you want, which you can then apply to the artwork.

Omnicrom or Color Tag: Another process allows you to add color to a black-and-white photocopy without creating expensive color transfers. Both Omnicrom and Color Tag use a special color film and heater that react with the toner on a laser photocopy. First, cut the color film slightly larger than the area you want colored, position it on the photocopy, and tape it in place. Then run the sheet through the Omnicrom or Color Tag machine and peel off the parent color film. The designated area should now be in color.

Photocopying methods: As the quality of photocopiers improves, the need for photostats for portfolio work decreases. Photocopiers today can copy onto a variety of materials— in black and white, color tones, and full color —at a fraction of the cost of the more traditional methods. If you have hands-on access to a good copier you will discover ways to get it to reproduce your work in many different ways. But even if you don't have one at your disposal, you might be able to find a quick-copy house with a cooperative operator who can help you with your portfolio needs. We will talk about the basic techniques first and then move on to the more exotic processes.

- **Straight copies:** Almost everyone in the art field knows how to make photocopies, but you can make better quality copies by following a few simple rules: keep the glass where you put your originals clean, make sure the machine has sufficient toner, find the exposure setting that works best for your needs, and experiment with the paper you are copying on. Trial and error will teach you a lot about the effects you can achieve.

- **Color copies:** Some photocopiers will print in different colors. These are usually color copiers with custom settings that copy one part in blue, another in green. But these effects have limited application. A more practical use of color copiers is enlarging and reducing full-color photographs, drawings, and slides for less than higher-quality photo prints would cost. Color prints and positives usually make better-quality photocopies than color slides or transparencies, although a skilled operator using a well-maintained machine can get remarkably high-quality photocopies from film source materials.

For color copies of color prints, your original is placed onto the copy glass, the reproduction size set, paper stock selected, and the copy made. The operator should adjust the color and exposure after seeing the result of the first print, which could be done while you wait. You can copy onto some color papers and specialty stock for unusual effects.

A color transparency needs to have a light source behind the image to transfer properly. Color slides are usually projected onto the copyglass through an attached slide projector. The image is sized through a zoom lens attachment, so you should specify how large you would like the image reproduced by giving the operator the dimension you want the final image to be.

- **Bubble-Jet prints:** Generally, color photocopies add contrast to your source materials but also lose subtle tonal ranges. If your colors are bright and clear, color photocopies will be adequate, but if you are working with pastel tones or more delicate shades, you may not be satisfied with the

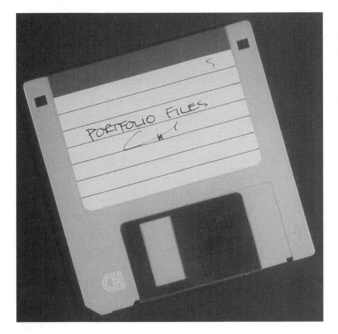

The day when entire portfolios are sent on computer disks is nearly here, but there will always be great appeal for design samples which can be held and inspected.

quality you can achieve this way. A new process called Bubble-Jet could be an option for you. It is less commonly available, usually through professional photo labs, and requires careful coordination with the operator. The tones you can achieve, however, are soft and delicate.

Computer Processes

Computers have revolutionized virtually all aspects of graphic design, from conception to execution. Never has it been easier to assemble and manipulate image and text, texture and color. Designers working with computers can take advantage of all the shortcuts this technology can provide as they create pieces for their portfolios. Generally, the most popular graphic programs available on computers include publishing programs like PageMaker and Quark, drawing programs like Freehand, Corel-Draw, and Illustrator, paint programs like Paint. CADD programs for architects, product designers, and interior designers, photo manipulation programs, and interactive media programs are constantly being developed and refined. They offer specialists in those fields endless opportunities not only to enhance their productivity but to demonstrate their talents to other colleagues and potential employers or clients.

In this book, we will stick to the basic graphic techniques for creating examples for your portfolio. Assuming you work with a computer, you have several common ways to input and output your work. You can scan source material, sketches, or roughs for further refinement and manipulation. You can create design work from scratch directly within the computer files. You can print to a laser printer in black ink on white or colored paper; you can send your files to a service bureau and have the work output at a higher resolution, either as positive or negative photo paper or as film prints; or you can have them output color files as color prints.

Output from a Linotronic printer, called "lino," is a high-quality black-and-white reproduction of your computer-generated files. You can modem your files or take them on disk to a typesetter or service bureau to have them printed. If your files include scanned halftones or line work, these elements should appear in scale and in place on the lino. Assuming that you know what you are doing and how to work with the service bureau, this process is quick, clean, and affordable.

Ways to Mount and Display Your Work

Binders

Three-ring: The most practical small binder is the three-ring notebook. It is available with many different kinds of covers, including cloth, plastic, leather, and metal. You can find three-ring notebooks in a variety of thicknesses, and the range of available accessories is impressive.

Binder accessories come in a great variety of materials; some are archival, others are not. Be sure you select the plastics that best show your work but will not damage it or deteriorate.

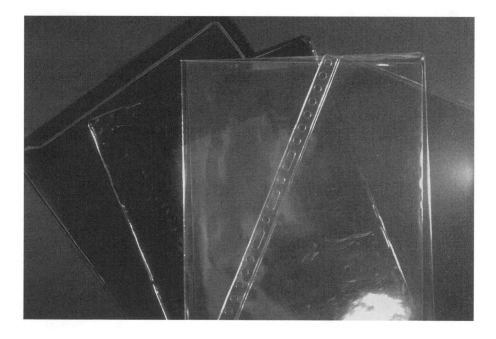

Multi-ring: The larger ring notebooks usually feature a multi-ring binding, with rings every half-inch. The choice of covering materials is more limited, but if you look through art-supply stores or mail-order catalogues, you should be able to find one to suit your taste. Accessories are also limited, but again there are some choices available by mail order. Cases are available in open or zippered styles, and come in many different sizes. We will discuss ways to create your own page, photo and slide protectors to suit your purposes.

Page, Slide, and Transparency Protectors

The three most common materials for page and photo protectors are mylar, vinyl, and

The best place to see samples of the different kinds of binder accessories is in a well-stocked camera store. This photographer stores his work in three-ring binders. A portfolio presentation for him is a simple matter of selecting slide sheets.

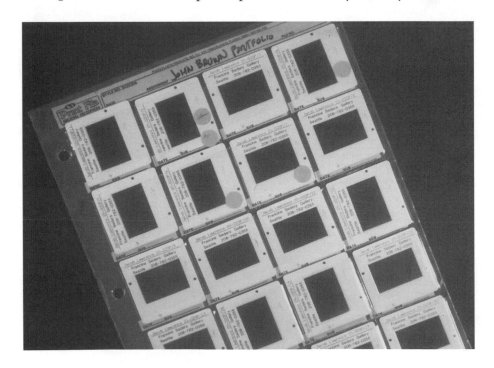

polypropylene. Mylar doesn't wear well, as it is stiff and tends to scratch and rip with rough handling. Vinyl is heavier and more flexible and is the clearest of the three. It is also available in clear front/frosted back styles for easier viewing of transparencies and slides. Insert the transparency so the viewer looks through the clear side to the transparency; the back light is diffused through the frosted side. A drawback, however, is that laser and photocopy toner tends to adhere to vinyl, especially if it is exposed to heat and pressure over an extended period. In addition to being archival safe, polypropylene is lighter weight and more flexible than either mylar or vinyl. Although not as clear as the other materials, polypropylene should be transparent enough for your portfolio purposes.

The selection of photo and transparency page protectors is amazing; there are now plastic page configurations for nearly every size and shape of photograph imaginable. While these protectors can be purchased for three-ring binders and storyboard portfolios, simply punch additional holes to tailor them to multi-ring binders. Protectors with pre-cut matboard can be purchased through mail-order sources.

Another way to protect and mount your photographs of artwork or flat printed samples is to have them laminated in plastic, leaving enough margin to punch holes for your binder rings. You can usually have items laminated through art supply stores, graphic arts services, and plastics suppliers.

Section Dividers

If you decide to organize your work thematically, you may want to create section dividers within your binders. You can do this with decorative papers, different kinds of plastic sheeting, film positives, or more unusual materials appropriate to your work. It is probably not necessary to spend a lot of time and energy on this element, however, since a change in theme is usually evident to the interviewer.

If your pieces are small enough, you can slip them into page protectors like this and store them in three-ring binders.

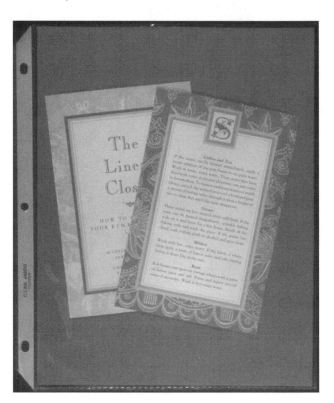

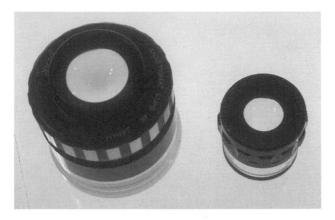

Loupes are essential for viewing slides and transparencies. Take one to each of your portfolio presentations.

Loupes and Slide Projectors

Most galleries, art directors, and design studios are used to reviewing work in slide form. However, if you include slides and transparencies in your portfolio, don't assume a slide projector, or even a loupe, will be available. Take a loupe along to the interview. Loupes come in many sizes, shapes, and degrees of quality. Select one that will work best with the size and format of your transparencies. If you have designed your portfolio for easy handling—with slide and transparency pages that can be lifted out and held up to a window or other light source— you shouldn't need to take a light box.

If you present your portfolio in your own office under your own projection conditions, a slide carousel portfolio can be impressive. But if you are going to the office of a client or potential employer and you have not been asked to present your work in this form, don't; setting up a slide-viewing area in a client's office could take more time than the interview itself.

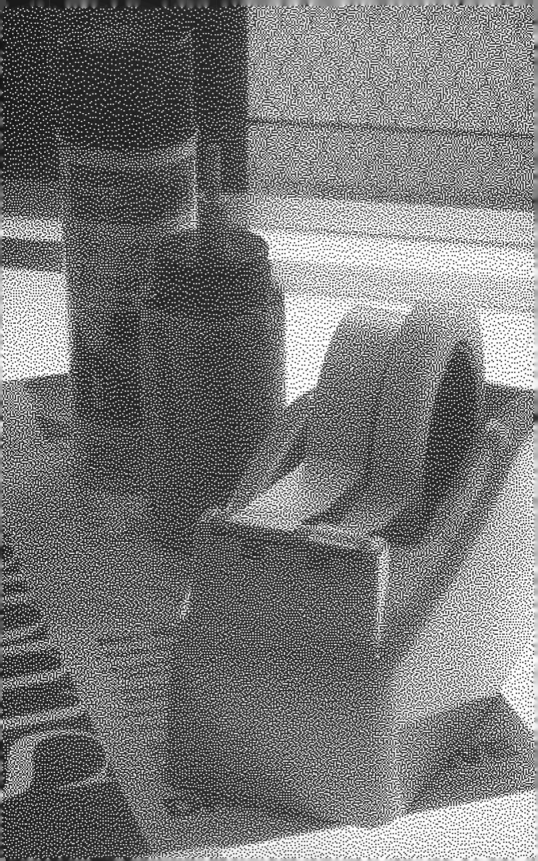

Chapter 4

Putting It All Together: Techniques for Assembling Your Portfolio

By now, your portfolio probably exists as bits and pieces of original artwork, photographs, photocopies, lino, loose transparencies, and stacks of slides. In this chapter we will discuss ways to mount and display these elements in ways that will show them off to advantage, while protecting them from the wear of frequent handling. We will discuss the most popular surfaces, like art papers, mounting board, and lamination. Then we will cover basic mounting adhesives and application techniques.

Mounting Surfaces

Art-Paper Mounts

If your portfolio is a binder style, you will need to mount your artwork on good, sturdy, medium-weight paper. There are many fine stocks to choose from, but the thin black paper sold with acetate protector sheets is not heavy enough. You should visit your art-supply store and check out their inventory of colored papers. Some have a forgiving texture that hides scuff marks. Durable, they are also available in a wide range of handsome colors. Other, uncoated,

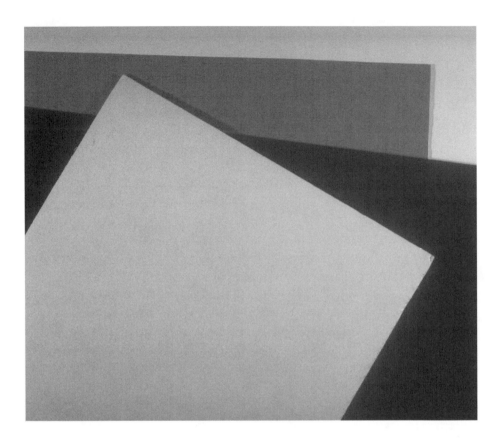

Pick a mounting board that shows your work off well, is sturdy enough to hold up over time, and is thin enough to fit in your binder or carrying case.

papers also come in attractive colors but are thinner and for most applications should be mounted on sturdier backing. Still other papers come in wonderfully rich colors, but their delicate surfaces scuff too easily for most portfolio applications. If you prefer white or cream stock for your mounts, you should consider watercolor paper, which comes in a variety of textures and weights and has the durability to withstand frequent handling.

Matboard and Foam Mounting Board

If you are preparing a storyboard portfolio, your mounts will probably need to be heavier than they would be in a binder, since you will be pulling out one piece at a time for your interviewers to inspect. Your mounts should be rigid, so you will want to consider using matboard, mounting board, or foam board.

Matboard: Used primarily by picture framers, this material, typically sold in 32 × 40" sheets, comes in a wide range of colors and textures. It can be found in most art-supply stores, although frame shops could probably order it for you as a courtesy. You will need to plan carefully how many mounts you will be able to cut from each sheet before you place your order. The most common thickness is about ⅛", but it comes in a double thickness as well. If you will be transporting your portfolio, you'll want to stick with the thinner sheets to avoid adding extra weight.

Mounting board: Similar to matboard in size and thickness, mounting board is sold only in white and black and has same-color core. It comes in 15 × 20", 20 × 30", and 32 × 40".

Foam board: Lighter than mounting board, but just as rigid, foam board comes only in solid white and solid black. At ³⁄₁₆" thick, bulk becomes more of an issue in your portfolio than weight, since only 10 sheets will fill out 2", which may be the limit of your portfolio case.

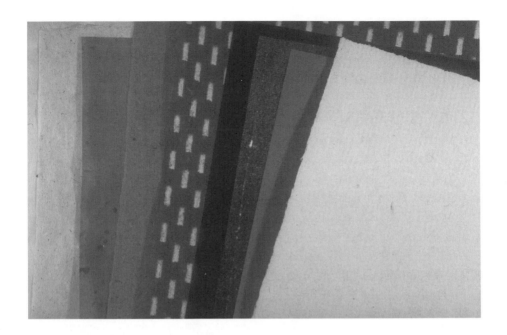

There are many wonderful and exotic papers available to brighten up your portfolio. Pick textures and colors that feature your work to its best advantage.

Lamination

A durable alternative to the bulk of matboard, mounting board, and foam board is to laminate your pieces between two sheets of heavy plastic. Of course, you won't want to do this with original artwork or with pieces whose surface texture it is important to see. But if you have many printed pieces to show, this might be the best approach for you.

Lamination is best with flat, thin pieces of smooth paper. You can usually get away with adding a layer of paper or rubdown type, but if the piece becomes too thick, with too many layers or with too much texture, you will end up laminating air pockets into this plastic sandwich, which is unacceptable. Five-mil clear vinyl is a good standard, but be sure to test the process first, using paper and materials similar to the artwork you want to mount, to make sure the effect matches your expectations.

You can use lamination in binders by leaving generous borders of plastic around the artwork, trimming it to the size of your binder, and punching holes into the binding edge to match the ring position.

Cutting Techniques

Since you will be spending a lot of money on these mounting materials, it is important to know how to cut them correctly so your edges and corners are straight and clean. If you are

Lamination is a fine way to protect printed pieces, but it does not work well with layered or textured surfaces. Experiment with different thicknesses of lamination and the process itself before committing one-of-a-kind pieces to the process.

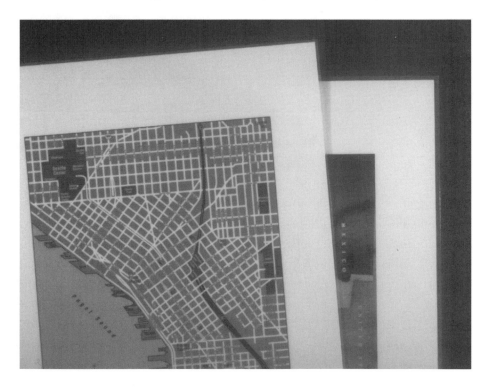

Paper cutters can give you good square cuts, if they are maintained. If yours is not, stick to sharp X-acto blades and T-squares for your portfolio pieces.

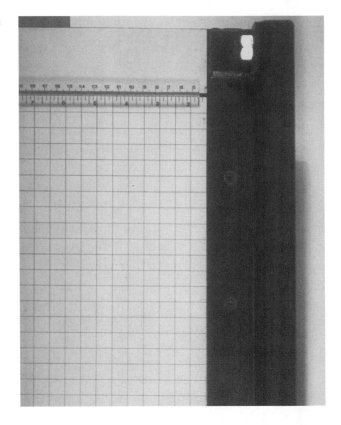

fortunate you will have access to a good, sharp, accurate paper cutter. Don't try to cut any more sheets at a time than the cutter can accommodate, and use any cutting rails and guides that come with the device.

If you don't have access to a good paper cutter, or if the blade is so dull it cuts curves in your board, you will need to make your cuts by hand. A T-square, ruler, triangle, and some tape are the tools you will need. Tape the board to your drawing board with some type of removable tape. (When you are ready to remove the tape, begin by peeling it away from the mounting paper, toward the drawing board. This will prevent ripping or tearing the paper.) Measure the board carefully and draw the borders with very light pencil lines. If your drawing board is a cutting surface, you can make your cuts directly with a mat knife or X-acto knife, using the T-square. The secret to cutting mounting board with straight edges and clean corners by hand is to follow these rules:

- Use a sharp blade.
- Cut on a soft surface like cardboard or rubberized cutting board.
- Hold your cutting edge firmly in place at the beginning and end of the cut.
- Keep your knife straight to the cutting edge, perpendicular to the item being cut.
- Lower the angle of the blade to expose more of it to the cutting edge of the paper.
- On thick board, make several *consistent* passes rather than trying to cut with a single stroke.
- Cut slightly past your corners.
- Make sure you have cut through the entire length of the cut before trying to separate the pieces.
- When cutting inside corners for windows, cut past the corner by about $1/16$". It's better to have small cut marks than ragged corners.

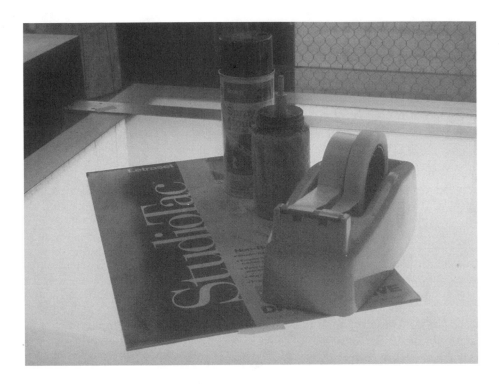

Experiment with your adhesive before using it on your portfolio pieces. Many are harmful to delicate artwork.

Adhesives

With all your mounts cut, you now need to consider the best way to attach the artwork. First, are you looking for a temporary, repositionable, or permanent mount? Do you need an adhesive at all? You may decide that designing a pocket or other holder for your artwork will provide the protection it needs without having to attach it permanently to a board or page in your binder.

Temporary mounts: With some engineering you may be able to devise pockets or corner holders to secure your pieces. The standard technique used by frame shops is to apply hinge mounts—flaps of thin paper and adhesive glued along the top edge of the artwork. This is the least damaging method of attachment.

You can also use double-sided adhesive tape, but you should realize that it is unlikely you will be able to successfully remove the tape once it is applied.

Repositionable adhesives: There are several spray adhesives on the market, including a range of products by 3M, that can be repositioned, but most of them are designed for more permanent mounts. StudioTac is a non-spray sheet adhesive that is repositionable (albeit with great care and effort once it has been firmly burnished down).

Permanent mounts: To be safe, you should consider all sprays and StudioTac permanent adhesives. The same goes for rubber cement, which has the additional problems of discoloring and bleeding through thinner paper over time. If you really want a permanent mount, have the piece professionally dry mounted at a frame shop or full-service art-supply store.

For all adhesives, follow the instructions carefully, paying particular attention to burnishing techniques and clean-up methods and to ventilation requirements for the spray mounts and chemical glues. Always test the adhesive to make sure it will work for your application before risking your artwork.

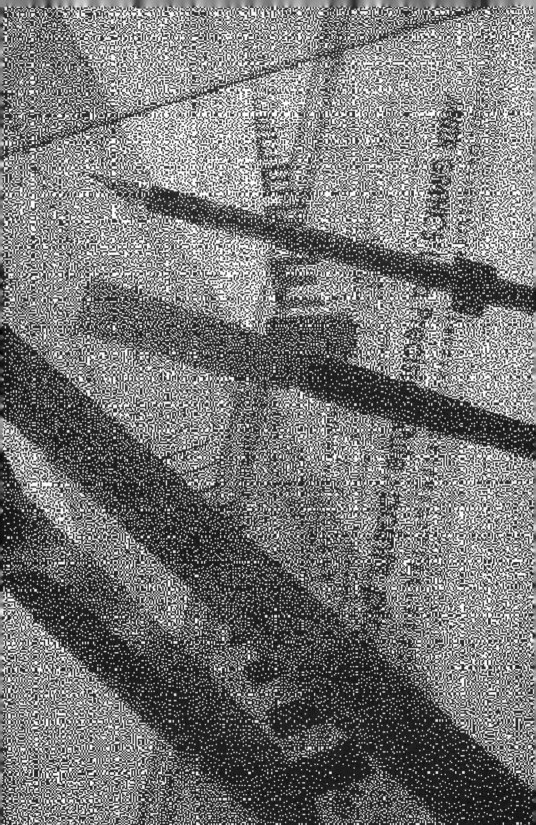

Chapter 5

Tightening Up Your Résumé and Leave-behinds

Résumé

A good résumé and cover letter are essential for job seekers. When trying to set up interviews with designers, you will often be told to send your résumé first. If they like what they see they will likely call you for an interview. If not, your résumé will probably be filed or tossed. This single correspondence might be your sole opportunity to get your foot in the door, so make it count. If you need help, don't hesitate to look in the library or bookstore for a book on résumé writing.

The best résumé is brief, specific, neatly designed, and well printed on good-quality stationery. Show some style, but not too much. The basic format is simple:

- name, address, telephone number (daytime and/or home)
- education
- work experience
- technical skills
- related interests, professional organizations, and affiliations
- references.

Name, address, telephone: These elements are simple enough. If you are changing jobs and don't want potential employers calling you at your current job, list your home number as the daytime telephone and be sure to have an answering machine picking up your calls. On your cover letter you can discreetly mention that you would like calls directed to your home telephone.

Education: In reverse chronological order, list degrees or certificates you have earned, followed by the school, your major and minor, and the terms and years you attended. If you have an advanced degree, include your thesis or dissertation topic. Include your high school degree if you have a two-year certificate from a community college or adult education program. If you have four years of college or more, drop it.

Work experience: Again in reverse chronological order, list previous employers, beginning with month and year, followed by the company name and your position and responsibilities. Don't list routine tasks that any employer would assume you would be able to do, such as photocopying, but do list more sophisticated tasks like filing, paste-up, computer work, reception, and preparation of presentation materials. On your résumé you don't need to include reasons for leaving previous jobs, but you should be prepared to answer those questions during an interview.

Technical skills: This section is essential. List any computer programs you are comfortable working with and any other specialized technical knowledge or training you might have. As more and more design work is being done on computers, it becomes increasingly important to show both basic and advanced familiarity with the major programs used by your profession. You don't need to include the version number of the software here.

Related interests, professional organizations, and affiliations: This section is where you let some of your personality come through. A reviewer will be able to create a better picture of your professional ambitions and interests with this information. Include data about specialized aspects of your field that you are actively developing. If you are in graphic design, say, and are particularly interested in typography or computer graphics, briefly mention this. If you are an interior design or architecture graduate with a particular interest in temporary shelter or furniture design, mention this. Professionally unrelated hobbies should be listed with caution; these can look amateurish. Languages and foreign study, on the other hand, should be included. Also list any professional organizations you belong to and any student or professional programs you have directed or participated in.

References: These are important. As a rule, employers' recommendations are more helpful than professors', but do include three or four of your most distinguished recommendations from professors. Just be sure they know you have included them and are willing to say good things about your abilities and work habits.

Ask them if they would allow you to include their telephone number on your reference list. If you are a student or recent graduate don't hesitate to include copies of letters of recommendation from instructors or previous employers. These may prove to be the determining factor in getting an interview.

Do not underestimate the importance of impeccable spelling and grammar on your résumé. Professional interviewers often circle spelling and grammatical mistakes, as well as organizational and typographic inconsistencies they find on résumés, and eliminate those with too many errors. They feel that if an applicant is not even willing or able to perfect a document as important as his or her own résumé, how careful will that person be in the work he or she does for the firm. It is a legitimate concern. Take the time and effort to comb through each detail of your résumé to make sure you have caught any potential snags. Ask others to review it too. It never hurts to have another set of eyes proofread the same information. You might be astonished to discover the obvious mistakes you were blind to.

Some job hunters find they have better luck getting interviews if they include a small photograph of themselves printed on the résumé. Since most résumés are so impersonal, this might be a good idea to help reviewers connect a person to the information.

If you are a graphic designer, avoid the temptation to turn your résumé into an exercise in corporate identification. Instead, make it simple, sharp, and typographically impeccable. If you are itching to show off your identity program skills, create portfolio pieces designed around more appropriate imaginary clients. If you are not a graphic designer, avoid the temptation to pretend to be one. Stick to good clean type and avoid anything cutesy or too "designed."

Finally, once you have your résumé as you want it, run off enough copies so you have plenty to distribute.

Leave-behinds for Freelancers

As a freelancer you probably won't need to include in your résumé as many details of your education, work history, and interests, or your recommendations from previous employers. You will, however, want to list your clients and the projects you have worked on. Your cover letter should indicate the kind of work you are seeking. If you are uncertain as to whether you are looking for regular employment or freelance assignments, include the full résumé information.

The well-established freelance designer, photographer, illustrator, architect, or interior designer should have something unusual to leave behind or send out. It may be a simple, well-designed reminder card, a photograph or photocopy of tear sheets of printed work, a promotional brochure, or a small poster. The most successful professionals, especially pho-

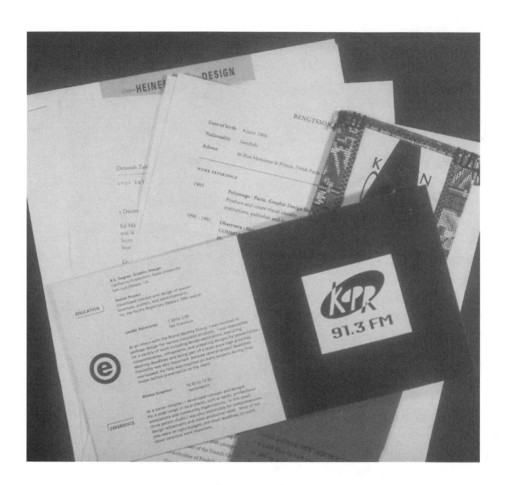

Résumés and leave-behinds for graphic designers should be concise, clear, and well designed. Use some imagination, but avoid over designing. Check spelling, punctuation, and style for consistency. Potential employers *will* look for errors.

tographers and illustrators, frequently mail out promotional pieces to ad agencies, art directors, design firms, potential and existing clients, and publications. It never hurts to keep your name—and a memorable image that you've created—in front of potential clients. Repetition is the key here. It is better to send out simple pieces frequently than to send something overly elaborate once with no follow-up.

Exhibition Histories for Fine artists

Fine artists looking for gallery representation or applying for grants or awards need a different kind of résumé than a job seeker. The fine artist's résumé should include:

- name, address, telephone number
- gallery or agent representation
- education
- awards, commissions, honors
- solo exhibitions
- group exhibitions
- bibliography.

Name, address, telephone number: This should be obvious.

Gallery or agent representation: If all of your professional correspondence and contact is handled through a representative, provide the reviewer with names, addresses, and telephone and fax numbers. If your work is managed by galleries, but you handle most of your business, list galleries by name and city only.

Education: List degrees or certificates, dates, and schools attended, from most recent to earliest. Do not include high school.

Awards, commissions, honors: List these with most recent first. A simple mention is more appropriate than a description of the honor.

Solo exhibitions: List these with most recent first. Give year, gallery or museum, city, and if a catalogue was produced, indicate that with a simple "Catalogue" at the end of each entry. This is not the place to discuss sales or prices.

Group exhibitions: List the same information as for solo exhibitions, but also provide the title of the exhibition. In either case, if the exhibition traveled, be sure to include a brief summary of the venues or time period.

Bibliography: If your work has been featured in reviews, articles, magazines, books, or exhibition catalogues or in other media, list these as well, again with most recent first. If you have an extensive bibliography, break the information into logical groups, like newspaper and magazine articles, books and exhibition catalogues, and so on.

A fine artist should keep all of this information in a computer file so that it can be updated regularly. Some galleries handle this for their artists, but often it makes sense for the artist to have backup files since he or she will usually be more knowledgeable about new information. Here again, spelling, style, and typographic consistency do count. You want the reader to notice your accomplishments, not your typos.

As a final note to fine artists, if a gallery or museum plans to produce an announcement card, brochure, poster, or catalogue, discuss getting additional copies *before* the piece is sent to the printer. You should also offer to pay for your additional copies rather than expect the gallery or museum to give you as many copies as you want. You might not think you should have to pay for run-on copies of these items— and you may be right—but in the end, these printed pieces, particularly the color ones, become invaluable promotional pieces if they are distributed wisely. And once again, settle this point with the gallery or museum *before* the piece has been sent to the printer.

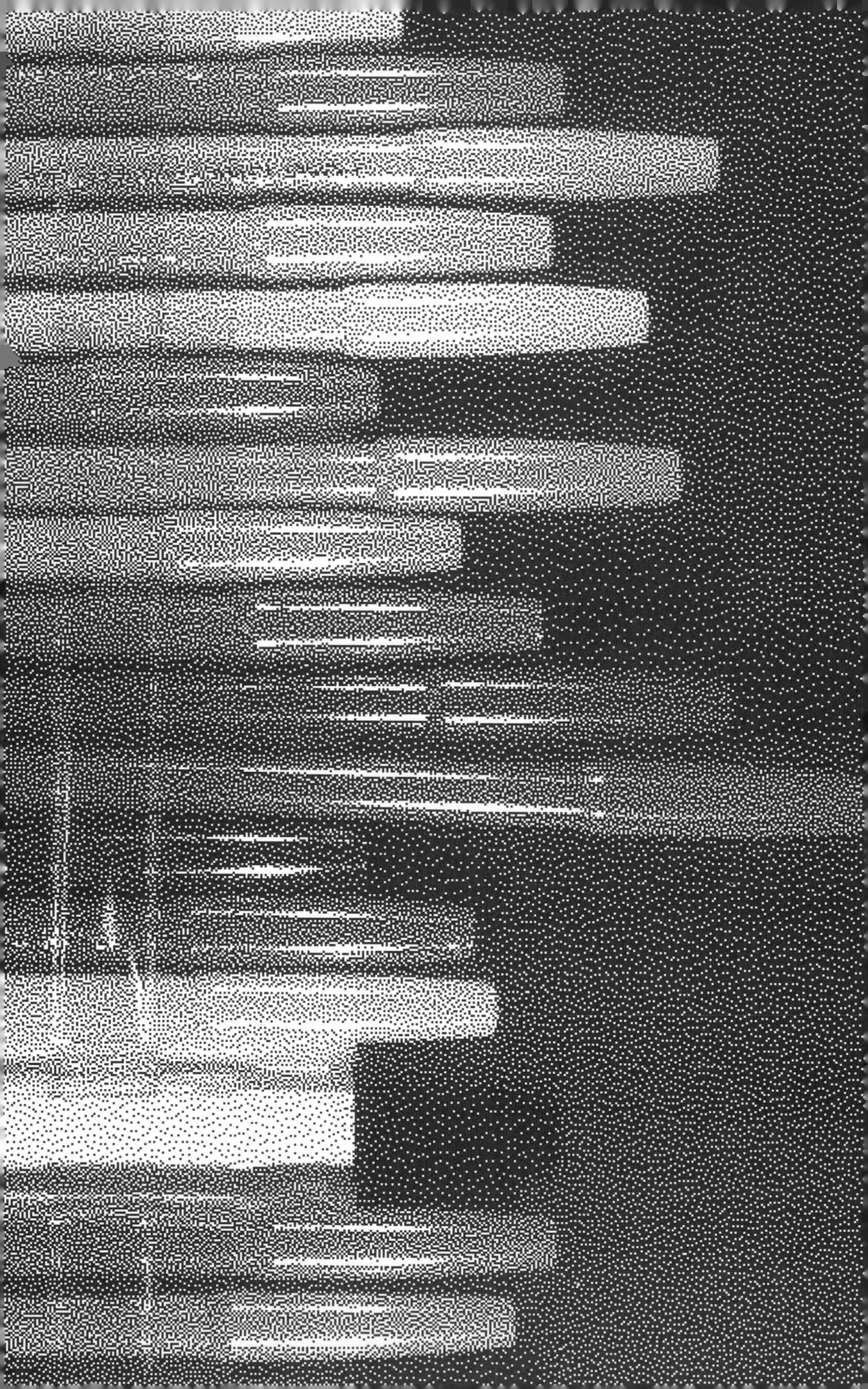

Presenting Your Work Effectively

Now that you've spent a lot of time and energy getting your portfolio in shape, it's time to show it off. In this chapter we will discuss ways to get interviews and portfolio reviews, how to prepare for and conduct yourself during an interview, how to follow up, and how to think about alternative ways to push the direction of your career.

Ways to Get Interviews and Portfolio Reviews

As discussed in the introduction, you will need to plan your strategy differently if you are looking for freelance work or gallery representation, but for now let's assume you are looking for a full-time design job. You are a recent graduate, and your portfolio is made up of one-third school assignments, one-third small personal jobs you have done on your own, and one-third new work created specifically for your portfolio. The word among your peers is that jobs are scarce and interviews are hard to get. What do you do?

Make a list of firms and individuals you would like to work for. This list should include the names of individual designers you can contact directly. For firms, especially larger firms, the contact person won't necessarily be the firm's principal; it will more likely be someone assigned to screen applicants. Obtain the name and title of the contact person from the firm's receptionist. Do some homework and try to learn who their major clients are and what kind of work they do. This information is harder to come by but might be available by reading design-award catalogues or asking around. (Don't pester the receptionist for this.) You want just enough information to get a sense of the kind of work they may need help with, so that you can tailor your cover letter and interview conversation accordingly.

Some job hunters prefer to send a letter first and follow up with a phone call, but others prefer to call first, follow with a letter, and then call again. In a competitive market you must be persistent, but you must never be rude. You might be turned down repeatedly by many firms. And some receptionists might seem abrupt in the way they respond to your requests for an interview; they are probably pestered more frequently than you can imagine. You might find it frustrating and even humiliating, but you must remember that you should not take an interview rejection as a personal offense. Remember, design firms are in business to make money, not to absorb young designers into the profession. Remember also that design firms tend to expand and contract with the workload, so a firm that is not looking for anyone one week might be desperate for help the next. Be persistent.

One underused technique for a job seeker who simply can't get a personal interview with a firm is to offer to leave his or her portfolio for review. Although this isn't as effective as a personal interview, at least it bears some potential. This might seem like a novel request to some smaller design firms, but larger firms only accept portfolios for review, granting interviews to those whose work seems to fit the firm's needs. This procedure saves staff time; most interviews last from 20 to 30 minutes, but a designer can quickly review a stack of portfolios in that same amount of time.

If you go this route, be sure you drop off your portfolio and pick it up again when you are told to. If you have any concerns about losing it at the firm, prepare a receipt for the receptionist to sign when you drop it off. Make sure your book is marked with a baggage tag or some other clear identification, including your telephone number. A firm may gather many cases to review in a single session, and an unmarked portfolio could be returned to the wrong designer.

You will improve the chances of a response to your work by leaving a brief cover letter, résumé, and evaluation note right inside the portfolio. This note should be checklist style, with simple questions like, "Does my work fit into any immediate or future projects you are working on?" "Would you like to set up an interview? If so, when?" "Are there any pieces in my portfolio you think are particularly strong or inappropriate for this group of work?" You might be inviting harsh response, but an honest impersonal evaluation is useful and leaves you with less doubt about the way the work was really received. And who knows, you might get some valuable advice or a lead to someone more appropriate.

Preparing for an Interview

Let's say your telephone and letter-writing campaign worked and you got several interviews. Before you go to your first one, rehearse your presentation. You might feel silly doing it, but it will help. Go to a quiet room by yourself, make note of the time, and rehearse. Pretend to introduce yourself to your interviewer, starting with typical small talk for a minute or two. Practice handing a résumé to the interviewer and discussing your background and employment interests. Be sure to indicate whether you would be willing to work part time or on call, in the studio or at your own home, or to freelance—but don't discuss money. Turn the discussion to the portfolio, opening it toward the interviewer. Turn each page and discuss each piece for a minute or two. Try to anticipate questions that might come up. Answer them concisely and then move on to the next piece. When you reach the end, ask the interviewer whether he or she has any questions. Finally, ask the interviewer if he or she has any work you might be suitable for. It takes some nerve asking this question, and it may seem pushy, but this does get to the heart of the reason for the interview. Look at your clock. If this exercise took longer than fifteen minutes, you need to speed it up by cutting out some of the chatter, or perhaps by editing out some of the artwork you are showing. Your actual interview should run about thirty minutes once your interviewer's questions and comments are factored in. Now do the whole thing at least one more time all the way through immediately. You will be surprised how much smoother and tighter the second time goes than the first. You might also discover changes you want to make in the portfolio itself.

When you arrive at the actual interview you should be on time, neatly and appropriately dressed. Don't overdress—go easy on the cologne, jewelry, and makeup—but don't underdress either. Even if a firm allows its employees to wear casual dress to the office, your interview is a formal situation. Your appearance and demeanor should be professional in every way, and you should seem confident and enthusiastic about your interview, your work, and your career.

When you meet your interviewer shake hands firmly. Look him or her directly in the eyes and introduce yourself clearly. The first few minutes are often the most nervous ones for inexperienced interviewees, and that's where the rehearsed small talk can come in handy. But if the interviewer wants to talk, don't interrupt. You want your interview to last about 30 minutes, the bulk of which should be focused on your work and abilities. In the unlikely event that the interviewer is talking about everything except you and your work, gently shift the conversation toward the portfolio.

Next, hand him or her a copy of your résumé and any recent letters of recommendation, preferably from former employers. Briefly highlight your most recent and relevant education and experience. Explain, just as you did in rehearsal, the nature of your interest and your availability. Open the portfolio and start discussing each piece as a design problem you solved. Give a one- or two-sentence description of the problem, and explain the resulting solution. If it is a piece you had only a part in producing, clearly describe the part you played. Never claim design credit for someone else's work; chances are you will eventually get caught. If you are nervous—and most interviewees are—you might be tempted to discuss each piece in either too much or too little detail. Avoid this temptation. Also, don't point out flaws or mistakes, but admit them if you are asked about them. Pick up cues from the interviewer, lingering or moving on as appropriate. Allow the interviewer to turn pages if he or she seems so inclined.

Resist the temptation to explain how difficult something was to produce, how long it took to do, or how many compromises had to be made along the way. This is student talk, which an interviewer hears all the time. It is usually boring and irrelevant to the success or failure of the final piece. It is appropriate, however, to explain which parts you would do differently next time, or how much you would like to get another assignment like it so you can take the concepts or production techniques a little further. That kind of talk is more professional, and more interesting.

If the interviewer is responsive to any piece in particular, try to engage him or her in some discussion about it. What do they like about it? How might they have handled something you had trouble with? Again, this is more professional conversation and will serve you better than acting inexperienced and insecure about your abilities.

When you come to a piece you created expressly for your portfolio, mention that. Say something like, "I wanted to show how well I could do this kind of project, so I produced these comps for my portfolio." At a minimum, this will show that you have more initiative than most of your classmates!

When you are through looking at the pieces, ask for a response. Does the interviewer have any work you can help with? Might there be something in the near future? Should you contact him or her again? If so, when? Does the interviewer have any leads or know of any opportunities you should investigate? It is surprising how often an interviewee fails to ask these questions, usually out of timidity. Your most important leads may come to you in the closing moments of an interview. Regardless of whether you received an unenthusiastic, or even sour, response, or whether your meeting went somewhat better, remain ever courteous, thank your interviewer for his or her time, and leave. Always send a thank-you note immediately after the interview. If the interviewer encourages you to follow up, do so promptly.

If you see an interviewer later at some public event or function, don't hesitate to reintroduce yourself and tell him or her your current job status. This is a good way to build a network of professional associates.

Special Types of Interviews and Portfolio Reviews

Freelance

A freelancer looking for occasional work or assignments isn't under the same pressures as a job seeker, but should approach the problem of finding employment with similar care. You will want to make a list of all of the firms that might have work for you and start to call. Frequently, firms or agencies will not make an appointment to speak in person to an illustrator, photographer, or designer until they have reviewed the prospective candidate's portfolio. As stated above, if you are concerned about leaving your portfolio unattended, have the receptionist sign a receipt for it. Encourage a specific response by enclosing a checklist-style comment sheet, and be prompt about picking up your book when the review is complete. Follow up with a letter, and add the firm to your marketing mailing list.

If you do get a personal interview, follow the same general rules as outlined above for job seekers. You want potential clients to think well of you. Dress appropriately, act professionally and enthusiastically, and try to develop a good rapport with anyone in the firm you might meet.

Fine Artist

Artists usually need only to contact a gallery and ask how one gets his or her work reviewed. Usually, the gallery manager will review transparencies and slides that are dropped off at the gallery. If there is further interest, arrangements can be made to view the actual work. Better galleries are pestered constantly by artists who show up unannounced, wanting to arrange studio visits or bring work into the gallery. Receptionist/gallery managers are often at the receiving end of this assault. They appreciate artists who show courtesy and good manners, regardless of whether the artwork is deemed appropriate for the gallery.

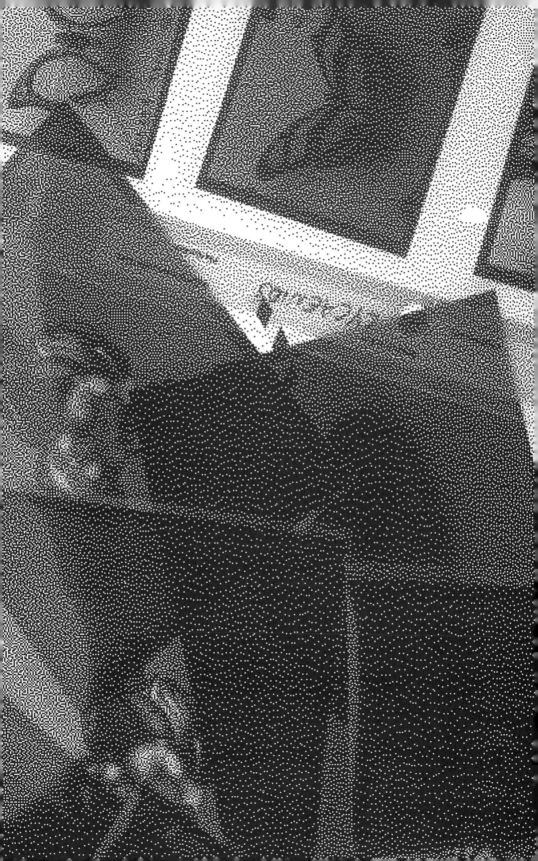

Chapter 7

Photographing Your Artwork

Unfortunately, few artists and designers work in a format small enough—or with materials flat, durable, or lightweight enough—to make practical portfolio pieces. The sculptor who works in bronze or cast fiberglass, the artist who paints on large canvases, the potter, the glassblower, and the weaver all share a similar problem—they can seldom show original work because it isn't practical or convenient. Artists who work in more contemporary forms, such as conceptual or performance art, don't even create tangible objects, which makes creating a portfolio considerably more complex. Architects, environmental planners, and interior, fashion, furniture, and industrial designers also need to convert their work to a size and format compatible with their portfolio. Probably the easiest and least expensive way to accomplish that is photographically.

Documenting Change and Preserving Work

Each artist works differently, of course, but some artists discover that the more involved they become in their profession, the more quickly their work grows and changes. By getting in the habit of consistently photographing your artwork, it's possible to illustrate your artistic growth—something that isolated pieces of artwork can't show. By successfully documenting and compiling examples of something as abstract as growth, you're putting your portfolio in a class apart from everyone else's. You have emphasized a creative direction, an important point in your favor that certainly should be shown in your portfolio.

Though any photograph of a piece of artwork is better than none at all, good photographs are considerably more helpful. Chances of the photograph being a good one are better if the photo is taken when the piece is in its best condition—usually when the piece is new. Delicate objects are frequently victims of careless handling or improper storage, and, often, even sturdy sculptural pieces never look as good as when they were just completed: wood cracks; paint discolors and peels; dings and chips from rough treatment occur. Some metallic work, aging gracefully and becoming patinated, does look better with age, but most work—especially contemporary work—looks better when it's fresh.

Another reason to photograph your artwork as soon as it's completed is that it might be your only chance. If the work is sold, you might never see it again. If the work is a drawing, print, painting, or fine illustration, it most likely will be framed and put under glass—making it all the more difficult to photograph.

Like artists, designers of all types are wise to photographically document their work.

Interior designers should photograph interiors immediately after finishing them, since they're often quickly changed by the client. Fashion and costume designers work with materials that are usually very susceptible to damage. If you make one-of-a-kind pieces, you have the same problem as artists who sell their work: it's entirely possible you'll never see your work again and never have an opportunity to photograph it.

Photography for most architects requires additional thought. You'll want photographs of your work at various stages of completion, with the final results well documented. Landscape architects and environmental designers often need photos taken over a long period to show how their work matures and changes with the seasons.

Slide Portfolios

Some art juries and most graduate schools review applicants' work in slide form. Sometimes they are very specific in their format requirements, asking that applicants send no more than, say, twelve slides. This process of evaluation by slides has advantages and disadvantages.

Obviously, a slide portfolio is inexpensive; mailing slides costs considerably less than shipping works of art. Also, slides are more convenient for both the artist and jury or committee members, especially when the work of many artists must be reviewed. If you're applying to

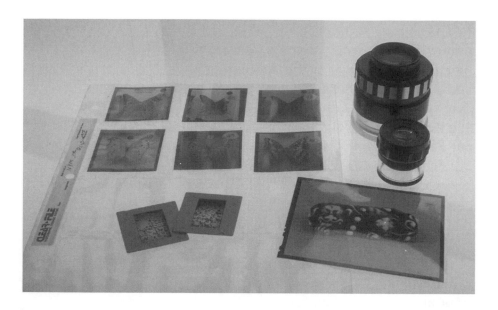

Slides and transparencies should be shown in slide pages or sleeves. Be sure to take a loupe to your interviews in case you need to point out important details.

several schools or competitions, you can mail duplicates of your slides to several places at the same time, which can be a real advantage. Slides can be great equalizers as well. Since each slide submitted will be viewed by each judge under the same circumstances, no one artist should start off with any great advantage. In theory, each artist is judged by the merits of the artwork alone, as represented by the slides.

Unfortunately, not every piece of artwork can be photographed with equal success. A beautifully subtle lithograph is likely to lose some of its flavor when photographed, while a massive bronze piece will reproduce fairly well in a slide. Visually bold and strong pieces tend to photograph better, and this is probably the chief disadvantage of judging artwork by slides.

As popular as the slide method of jurying is now, it will probably become standard practice in the years ahead. If you're applying for graduate school, entering a contest, or submitting your slides for whatever reason, the following steps can help you improve your chances:

- Send only your very best slides.
- Send slides that accurately represent your work. Juries frequently do their initial selection by slides and their final jurying from the original work, and judges do not hesitate to reject work that was inaccurately represented in the slide.
- Clearly mark your slides with complete caption information and correct orientation. Also, include a written list of this information so that a judge can read it while looking at the projected images.
- Clean and dust your slides before sending them.
- Avoid sending slides in glass mounts, since some projectors cannot accomodate them.
- Mask out distracting background details, using metallic mylar tape especially made for the purpose.
- Package your slides securely to protect them during shipping, e.g., in plastic slide protector pages sandwiched between two sheets of cardboard.
- Include a stamped, self-addressed return envelope to ensure they will be returned promptly after jurying.

- Whenever possible, send good-quality duplicates; if you must send the originals, keep duplicates for yourself. Never send your only copy of an important slide.
- Try to shoot a three-dimensional object from an angle that best describes the piece, but send more than one view if that's what it takes to represent the piece fairly. This is as important for architectural models as it is for sculpture.
- When one slide of an entire piece doesn't do the work justice, send close-up detail slides. Clearly mark them as such so they won't be judged as separate entries.
- Before you mail them, always project your slides or carefully inspect them with a loupe to check for clarity, focus, and general impact. Flaws are much more noticeable in slides when they're projected than when they're just held up to a light.
- Keep a record of when and where you send your slides so you can locate them if they aren't promptly returned. Slides are small enough to be easily misplaced and forgotten, so you may need to send a reminder to get them back.

Getting Ready to Photograph

If you produce flat artwork like paintings, prints, drawings, floorplans, sample boards, or graphics, and if you know you're going to have to photograph them regularly to get slides or enlargements for your portfolio, you might decide to set aside a corner of your studio as a photo area.

Basic Photo Equipment

The basic photo equipment you'll need includes: camera, film, tripod, cable release, light meter, gray card, lights, reflectors, light stands, backdrop paper, and miscellaneous items.

Camera

An increasing number of design departments in colleges and universities require that their students learn to take good photographs with 35mm cameras. Most insist on 35mm cameras for several reasons:

- they're extremely versatile;
- film, lenses, filters and accessories are widely available;
- the quality of the photography can be very good; and
- although the camera itself can be expensive, film and processing costs are reasonably priced.

If you have a 35mm camera, it can be one of two kinds: a range finder or a single-lens reflex ("SLR"). With an SLR model, when you look through the viewfinder, you're looking through the actual lens of the camera. Whatever you frame in your viewfinder will be on the film when you trip the shutter. An SLR is easier to use than a range finder because each time you change lenses or add filters, your eye sees what the film will capture.

With range finder cameras, on the other hand, when you look at your subject, you look through a window that shows you approximately what the film will record. If you change lenses or add filters, you must imagine how that is going to affect the shot. Still, if you have a range finder camera, you should be able to take acceptable photographs of your artwork.

If you're about to buy a camera, you should give serious consideration to an SLR model for these reasons: First, you'll probably find SLRs much easier to learn to use. Second, if you plan to photograph very small objects, such as jewelry, you must be able to see exactly what will appear on the film, and this is only possible with an SLR.

If you're a jeweler or if you do other very small work, you will need a macro lens or set of close-up lenses. With a macro lens you can take extreme close-up shots as well as regular shots, ranging from normal distance to infinity. With close-up lenses, you attach one over your regular lens whenever you want to take a picture a few inches from the subject.

Film

There are a variety of films on the market in the two most basic types: black-and-white and color. It's important for you to know what to expect from each so that you can select the film most appropriate for your needs.

Black-and-white films: Most black-and-white films are negative acting, which means that you get a transparent negative image when the film is developed. It is from these negatives that prints or enlargements are made. Prints can be as small as the individual frame on the film itself or as large as a wall mural. For portfolios they usually range from 5 × 7" to 11 × 14" and can be as large as 14 × 22".

Each type of black-and-white film has important characteristics. Some are fast, meaning they don't require much light to become fully exposed. Although these films are handy in low-light situations without a flash, they tend to be grainy, and enlarged prints from grainy film show a sandy texture on the surface of the subject. Some photographers work for grainy effects, while others feel they distract from the real image. Kodak's Tri-X is a fast film; it has an American Standards Association speed rating ("ASA") of 400.

Other films are very slow, meaning that it takes a lot of light to fully expose them. They're most often used outdoors on bright days. Their chief advantage is that because they are fine-grain films, they can be blown up to much greater proportions without producing a distracting texture. Kodak's Panatomic-X falls into this category. A very slow film, it's rated ASA 32.

In the middle range, with fairly fine grain, is Plus-X. At ASA 125, it's fast enough for most normal lighting situations, both indoors and out. This versatile film is a good one for most amateurs to use to photograph their artwork.

Color films: Working with color film can be more complicated, only because color is such a variable element. Since color is determined by the light in which it's seen and since types and sources of light vary dramatically, a single type of film will not satisfactorily reproduce every kind of color in every kind of light.

For accurate color reproduction, you need to match the film to the light source. Daylight film is used when the primary source of light is the sun or a flash or strobe light. Tungsten film is used when the primary light falling on the subject is tungsten or incandescent light. Although the variation in colors effected by these types of light is not readily discerned by the human eye, it is markedly recorded on film. Color photos taken with unfiltered fluorescent light often come out looking extremely blue-green, as do daylight shots taken with tungsten film. The opposite happens when daylight film is used in tungsten light. The colors come out much too warm in tone: whites are replaced with deep yellow, and blues nearly disappear.

The only way to accurately photographically reproduce the colors in your artwork is to match your film to the ambient light and to avoid photographing under fluorescent light whenever possible. Filters that convert fluorescent light to daylight- or Tungsten-light temperatures are available. But the results are usually less than satisfactory, primarily because there are too many kinds of fluorescent bulbs to allow for easy matching of filters to bulbs.

Both daylight and Tungsten films are available in slide and negative forms. Slide film is a direct positive film, meaning that what you put into your camera is what you get back from the photo lab mounted as slides. Print film is a negative film, meaning that positive prints are made from the negative film you put into your camera. You can tell which kind of film you're buying by the endings in the brand names: the suffix "chrome" used with any color film indicates that it is slide film, while the suffix "color" indicates negative film. Thus, Ektachrome, Kodachrome, and Fujichrome are all slide, or transparency, films, while Kodacolor and Vericolor are negative, or print, films.

Tripod

Tripods are required for all exposures taken at more than ⅓₀th of a second, and because the photography of artwork requires long exposure times, you'll need a tripod to hold your camera steady. Inexpensive tripods are usually very lightweight and unsteady; they jiggle during exposures. But suspending a jug of water from the neck of the tripod will make it steady.

Cable Release

A cable release prevents jiggling the camera when you press the shutter. One is necessary for tripod shots.

Light Meter

There are two types of light meters: incident meters, which have a Ping-Pong ball–like sphere attached to them, and reflective meters, the type frequently built into cameras but which, like incident meters, can also be purchased as handheld models. Although incident meters are probably easier to use, a less-expensive reflective meter will work well for artwork as long as it is used in conjunction with a gray card.

Gray Card

An 18 percent gray card will help you get more accurate color in your color slides. They cost a couple of dollars and are available in larger camera stores.

Lights

As mentioned earlier, the lights you use must be rated at the same color temperature as the color film you are using. For example, if you use Ektachrome 50, a good film for photographing artwork, you'll be using a film balanced for 3200° Kelvin light, which means that your light bulbs should be rated to 3200° K. (With tungsten films, a 3200° K light source must be used to achieve accurate color rendition. Other photo lights, such as strobe lights and flash bulbs, are balanced for daylight films. The advantages of 3200° K bulbs are their relatively low cost and the fact that you can see their light—and thus have more control—

because they remain on, while strobes or flashes are on for only an instant.) Camera stores usually stock, or can order, inexpensive screw-in type light bulbs that have a color temperature of 3200° K. They don't last for more than a few hours, so don't use them as regular light bulbs and do keep replacements handy.

Reflectors
Aluminum bowl reflectors with grip clamps on the back are available in hardware stores for a few dollars each. The grip clamps allow you to use chairs, tables, and bookcases as convenient light stands.

Light Stands
For infrequent use, crudely fashioned light stands made from 1 × 2" strips of wood about 6 feet tall and attached to a sturdy base will do very well.

Backdrop Paper
Seamless photo paper, sold in 10-foot-wide rolls, is the standard professional backdrop material; however, you might feel it is too expensive for infrequent use. If a white or brown backdrop is adequate, butcher paper or brown wrapping paper in a 6- to 10-foot length will provide you with a very inexpensive backdrop. Many amateur photographers make the mistake of getting too arty or textural with their backgrounds. Backdrops should be entirely subordinate to the artwork itself, so choose

your backdrops carefully. Textured fabrics, such as velvet, burlap, and satin can look gaudy and unnecessarily dramatic. Generally, smooth mat fabrics and papers in neutral or subdued colors will enhance your artwork. Objects or artwork with fine detail or subtle tonal changes often benefit from very dark backdrops, and architectural mockups convey more realism when they are photographed against backgrounds that approximate those of the actual site: sky blue, grass green, concrete or asphalt gray, and so on.

Miscellaneous Supplies

On your list of supplies, you should include masking tape, pushpins, clamps, staples, or whatever it takes to hold your work in place while you photograph it. If you're shooting three-dimensional objects you'll need a piece of white cardboard or cardboard covered with aluminum foil to reflect light onto any distractingly harsh shadows, and if you're shooting small objects you'll need a table about waist high or lower to set them on while you photograph them.

If you're shooting with color film, you'll want only Tungsten light, so you'll need to purchase some Rubylith or heavy black paper to block sunlight from your photo area. (If it's not practical to block out the light, you'll have to shoot your slides at night, when natural light is no longer a problem. You'll also need to turn off all fluorescent lights while you're shooting.)

With black-and-white films, you can use any combination of light sources without affecting the results.

Photographing Flat Objects

Unless your work is very small, it's usually easier to photograph flat artwork on a wall rather than on the floor, especially since most tripods aren't adjustable or flexible enough to be positioned so that the legs don't appear in the picture frame. Find a wall that has as much unobstructed space in front of it as possible. If you're photographing a stretched painting, you'll want to use a wall on which hardware for hanging can be installed.

1. Prepare the artwork: First, remove the artwork from any frame, glass, or mat. Then, hang, tack, or tape it low enough on the wall so that the center of the artwork is as high as the lens of the camera on the tripod.

2. Position the lights: If your artwork is small, flat and without texture, you should distribute the illumination evenly over its entire surface, to eliminate hot spots, dark areas, and harsh shadows. Remember that the farther the lights are from the artwork, the more even the illumination will be. You also want to keep the height and angle of the lights and their distance from the artwork consistent with each other.

To determine the proper position for your lights, find the vertical center line of your artwork, bring that line down to the floor, and

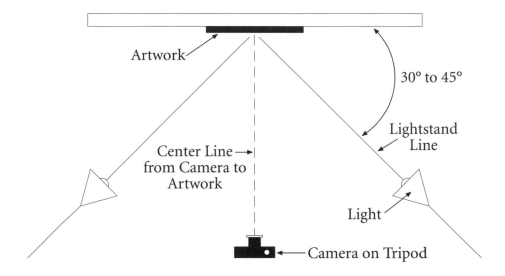

The diagram above shows how to position your photo lights and camera when shooting flat artwork mounted on a wall. The diagram below shows how the lights should cross over the painting to get more even illumination. To avoid hot spots, aim your lights to opposite sides rather than pointing them at the center.

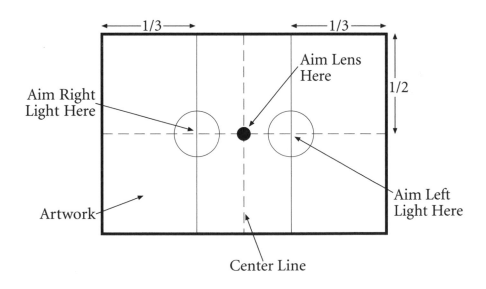

continue it along the floor (your camera will be centered along that line). Next, bisect at 45 degrees the two 90-degree angles formed at the intersection of the floor line and the bottom of the wall and bring those lines out from the wall. Position your lights along these lines at equal distances from the artwork, so that a line from one light to the other is parallel to the wall. Now, raise your lights level with the center of your artwork, and then do the same with your camera lens.

With your lights in proper position, aim them so they bathe the surface of the artwork with light. If you were to aim both lights at the center of the artwork, you would have a photograph with a bright center and dark edges, which isn't what you want. Instead, aim the light on the right side of the picture to a point approximately one-third of the way in from the left edge of the artwork; aim the left light at a point one-third of the way in from the right edge. If your lights are far enough from the artwork (and you have carefully placed them as described), your artwork should be evenly illuminated.

3. Check the lighting: To test for even lighting, tack or tape a sheet of plain white, brown, or gray paper over the entire artwork. Take your light meter or camera (if you're using the light meter built into your camera) and hold it about 6 inches from the paper cover. Move the light meter slowly across the entire surface of the artwork, watching carefully to see if the needle on the light meter changes position. If it does, then one section of the artwork is receiving more light than the other, and it will appear as a hot spot in the finished photo. Reposition the lights and test again.

Test the light carefully, because although it's difficult for the human eye to accurately distinguish between even and uneven illumination, the difference will be obvious in the finished photograph. If you're using an incident (or Ping-Pong ball–type) meter, you won't need to cover the artwork with paper. Instead, point the white sphere toward the camera lens and move the meter back and forth across the artwork, again watching to see whether the needle moves. Once you've determined that the artwork is evenly illuminated, remove the paper cover and take your light reading from the 18 percent gray card.

4. Determine the exposure: If you're going to use your camera's light meter to determine the exposure, you should take a light reading before you position your camera. Set the f-stop on your camera to its smallest setting: f16 or f22. Then, take your camera and gray card up to the artwork and, holding the card (gray side toward the light) parallel to and a few inches in front of the work, take a light reading with the camera about 6 inches from the gray card. Adjust the shutter speed, rather than the f-stop, to the proper exposure. Remember this reading, because as long as your lights remain in the same position, you will use it to shoot all the artwork you have ready. If you move the lights, you'll need to take another reading and adjust the camera accordingly.

If you're using a handheld reflective light meter, take the gray card and the light meter up to the artwork. Hold the card in front of the artwork and point the light meter at it to take the light reading—you want to know how much light is reflecting off the gray card. Using the smallest f-stop your camera has, set your shutter speed to what the light meter indicates will give you the proper exposure. You should take the reading with a gray card rather than from the artwork itself, because you want to know how much light is hitting the artwork rather than how much light is reflecting off it. Incident light meters measure this automatically, since they measure light hitting the subject rather than bouncing off it. With an incident light meter, point the white sphere toward the lens, take the reading, and adjust the camera accordingly. You'll want to shoot using long exposure times and small f-stops to give the maximum depth of field and the sharpest edges possible on the artwork.

5. Square the camera: The next step is to set the camera in front of the artwork, squared, centered, and positioned so that the artwork is properly framed in the viewfinder. Take the time to do this step properly, because unless you square the camera to the artwork you will get a trapezoidal image instead of a rectangular one.

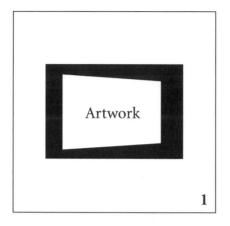

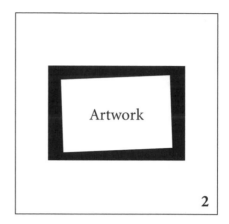

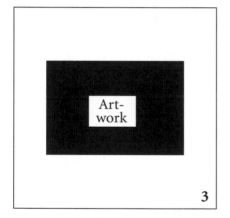

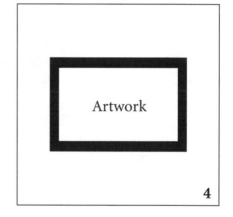

Slides one through three show how not to frame your artwork as you photograph it. Slide four shows the correct position.

To center the image, you must position the lens to the center of the artwork. The most accurate way to do this is to position the camera directly over the 90-degree line you established when you positioned the lights. Move the camera along that line until the artwork is comfortably positioned in the viewfinder. If the image is tilted, adjust the tripod, camera, or both until the artwork is square in the viewfinder.

Finally, tighten any adjusting screws on your tripod to keep the camera in place; be careful not to move the camera in the process.

6. Shoot the photos: When you're satisfied with the way the image is positioned in the viewfinder, recheck your exposure and make sure the camera is correctly focused. Shoot the photo by carefully squeezing the cable release without jiggling the camera.

If you're shooting slides, expose at least as many frames as you will need slides. If you're making negatives, either color or black-and-white, it's always a good idea to bracket your exposures. Bracketing means you shoot one frame that according to your light meter is a little overexposed, one frame just as your light meter tells you, and one that's slightly under-exposed. Following this method, you can be certain that at least one of the three shots will be accurate, even if your light meter isn't absolutely accurate or if your camera shutter is a little slower than it's supposed to be.

Bracket by moving the f-stop one setting past or one setting before the proper setting, or by changing your shutter speed by one setting each way. For example, let's say you want three perfect slides of a drawing and your light meter indicates that the proper exposure is f22 for a quarter second. You would first shoot three exposures at f22 for one fourth of a second, then you would move the shutter speed to one eighth of a second, keeping the f-stop at f22. Finally, you would change the shutter speed to half a second at f22 and shoot three more exposures. The results should be nine slides, three properly exposed, three under-exposed, and three slightly overexposed.

Bracketing is the easiest way to make sure you have compensated for minor inaccuracies in the film or your photo equipment; it's a standard practice among professional photographers. Amateur photographers object to bracketing because it seems like such a waste of film; but shooting six shots more than you need to get three good ones is not truly expensive, especially if you want excellent photographs of your artwork.

7. Prepare for the next shot: You can save yourself a lot of preparation time on subsequent shots if you have artwork that's the same size as the previous, so that it can be placed in exactly the same position. Until the artwork changes size (or until you have to re-position the lights) all of your initial adjustments can remain the same.

Shooting Flat, Textured Objects

If you have an embossed print, weaving, bas relief, or other piece of textural artwork, you probably want the texture emphasized rather than flattened in the photos. To bring out the texture, move one or both of the lights closer to the wall so that the light rakes the surface of the artwork and creates more distinct shadows.

Carefully check the results of your lighting arrangement in the viewfinder. Slight changes in the position of the lights can dramatically alter the way the texture of the piece appears. You may discover that by raising one of the lights, the texture becomes more pronounced. Perhaps by moving one light back a little, a section of the texture becomes less noticeable. With artwork that is textured but flat you have to play with the lights as though you were shooting a three-dimensional object. Watch carefully how the light works with your piece and you'll learn what kind of lighting setups are best for your objects.

Difficult Flat Pieces

In some ways it's harder to get a good photo of a flat object than of a sculptural one. Dark pencil lines, heavily varnished paintings, flat display boards with many photos, and different kinds of textures all reflect light in a way that's difficult to photograph. You'll have to move the lights around until the reflections are softer, smaller, or not noticeable. For some work, polarizing camera filters will help reduce the reflections, and for extreme reflection problems, polarizing filters for your lights are available. If you want to take good photographs of reflective artwork but can't afford expensive equipment, you must become proficient at positioning your lights.

Flat pieces that are too large to properly illuminate in the studio can be successfully photographed outside using black-and-white or daylight color film. Slightly overcast days provide more even illumination. Photograph around noontime, and the color rendition of your color photos and slides will be more accurate. Keep in mind, however, that it's difficult at any time to get accurate color rendition out-of-doors.

Photographing Three-Dimensional Objects

Photographing three-dimensional art objects is a profession all its own, full of subtleties, techniques, and years of training. However, if all you want to do is take good, accurate slides and photographs of three-dimensional work without spending a lot of money on special equipment, don't be discouraged—it isn't difficult to learn to take good photos using inexpensive equipment in a primitively arranged studio. About the only differences between photographing three-dimensional objects and flat objects are the composition of the image within the frame and the lighting of the object.

Since light determines how the eye perceives an object, you can alter an object's form by altering the way light hits it. With art objects, you want accurate representations of the work, and therefore you will want a lighting setup that emphasizes the shape of your subject without exaggerating or distorting it.

To properly photograph a three-dimensional object, you'll need at least three lights. The "key" light is your main light. A "fill" light is usually placed so that it fills the harsh shadows created by the key light. The "shadow," or background light, illuminates the background the object is resting on and thereby determines how the rest of the composition will work. All three lights are important, so watch how each affects the entire picture.

Aluminum foil reflectors make excellent, inexpensive fill lights by reflecting light from one of your main lights to the area of the piece you want to highlight. Clamp-type reflectors are handy because they can be clamped to bookcases, chair backs, or anything else that can serve as a light stand. The more maneuverable your lights are, the better control you will have on the lighting of the art.

If you're shooting black-and-white film, you can use any combination of lights available—daylight, fluorescent, small desk lamps, and even flashlights. Color shots will require 3200° K lights and tungsten film if you want accurate color.

For a natural-lighting effect, you'll have to place the lights above eye level, since most natural light comes from above. Fill and highlight lights can shine from below so as to bring out details in shadowed areas.

Most art objects look best when photographed on a sheet of seamless backdrop paper that is tacked to a wall and draped in a gentle curve over the photography table. Properly positioned and framed in the camera, the object will look as though it were in a color field, uninterrupted by horizon lines and seams.

For color work, subdued color backgrounds are more flattering to most pieces than brilliant or garish backgrounds. As a rule, select background colors as you would choose colors for mats for flat artwork, avoiding heavily textured backgrounds. Rules of contrast apply here too. A dark object will separate itself from a lighter background just as a light object will show up more distinctly when photographed on a darker background.

Place your object on the seamless paper and then decide from which angle it should be lighted and photographed. Move the lights around, changing their heights and distances until you've found the most satisfactory setup. Keep in mind that you're trying to get an accurate photograph of the artwork. Avoid overly dramatic or theatrical lighting.

Once you have the artwork and background properly lighted, and the shadows working with the piece, you must determine what exposure setting to use. Put the gray card in front of the object and place your camera within a foot of the object and card. If you're using a handheld reflective light meter, hold it a foot from the gray card. If you're using an incident meter, hold it in front of the object, with the white sphere pointed toward the camera lens. Be careful not to shadow the light meter or gray card while determining the exposure.

Since you will want to position your camera close to the object yet keep as much of it in focus as possible, use f16 or f22 and adjust your shutter speed accordingly. Those settings will provide the greatest possible depth of field.

Framing the object in the camera is the last step before taking the picture. Position your camera and tripod far enough away from the object so that it doesn't look crowded in the viewfinder, yet close enough so that the details of the artwork are visible. Logically, if you're shooting an object that is taller than it is wide, you should shoot the photograph vertically and vice versa for pieces that are wider than they are tall.

Compose your photograph carefully. When looking through the viewfinder, take an extra moment to think about how you're lighting and framing each shot, and visualize how the finished photo will look. Film and processing for 35mm cameras are not so expensive that you can't afford to experiment. Take many more shots, with different lighting setups, than you actually need, and you're more likely to end up with at least one excellent shot of your artwork. Again, remember that photography of artwork is its own art form. If you are interested in the field, ask a professional photographer to recommend a book or check your library or bookstore for titles on this interesting specialization.

Processing, Editing, and Storing Photos and Slides

It's common practice for amateur photographers to drop off a roll of black-and-white film at a camera store and get back 20 or 36 black-and-white 3 × 5" prints. It also commonly occurs that the results are disappointing. When black-and-white film is sent to a large lab, a machine usually develops the prints; the results are generally uniform but of mediocre quality and not very flattering to your subject.

Working with Contact Sheets

Another method of working with black-and-white and color films is to request that the lab develop the film and provide you with a contact sheet. In addition to your negatives, you will receive a large sheet of photo paper with small prints of your negatives. From this contact sheet you can select the most successful shots and decide which ones you want enlarged to 5 × 7" or 8 × 10" prints.

First, indicate on the back of the contact sheet which images you want enlarged by writing the numbers of the negatives and any specific instructions. Then return the contact sheet and the negatives to the photo lab. Photographs chosen and printed this way will be of higher quality, and since you can include cropping instructions, they'll have more balanced composition as well.

Correcting and Editing Your Slides

When your slides have been returned by the photo lab, go through them carefully. Put them into a projector or viewer or, better yet, spread them out over a light table and inspect them with a loupe. The first thing you should be looking for is how good the slides look overall. If your exposure is consistently good, the focus is clear, and the color is coming out well, you know that the way you're shooting your photos is working and you can go on to look for the finer qualities in your slides. If you aren't getting consistently good results, you'll have to find out why.

If your slides are consistently too dark, you're underexposing them. If they're too light and washed out, you're overexposing them. If the image is blurred, you're jiggling the camera as you press the shutter, or your subject is moving, or your shutter speed is too slow. If you can't figure out what the problem is, it's a good idea to buy a roll or two of film and experiment with exposures, shutter speeds, and lighting conditions, carefully recording how you shot each slide. Check the results against your notes and you should have a good idea of what is happening to your photos.

If you find yourself generally frustrated with the results of your photos, find a beginning photography book and go through it carefully, checking your knowledge of photography against the book; it's good practice for any photographer. There are many excellent, simple, and easy-to-understand photography books available in camera and book stores and in libraries. Textbooks used in basic photo classes in college can be especially helpful to the amateur. When you are satisfied with the general quality of your slides, you are ready to direct your attention to the more subtle details.

First, if you are editing a roll of slides using a loupe and a light table, throw away the obviously unusable ones—the dark, blurry, or washed-out ones. Also discard any with a skewed orientation. Check closely to see that your entire subject appears on the slide—that you didn't cut it off at the top, bottom, or sides. Make sure the subject fits comfortably within the frame and isn't overwhelmed by too much space around it, by too many background details, or by a distracting film box or camera strap that was inadvertently left in the frame when you shot the picture.

After you've thrown away the unusable slides, inspect those you have left. If you took more than one slide of each subject, or if you bracketed your exposures, select the one from each set that seems the very best—the clearest, sharpest, and truest in color. Put it in a stack of your best shots and put your second choices in a separate pile. Retain the best slide of each piece for your files and use the duplicate or second shots to enter shows, to send to colleges, or to give to artist or design registry files. If you know at the time you're taking the pictures that you will need several slides of the same piece, take the extra shots then rather than making duplicates from your one good original. There are two reasons for doing it this way: you get better quality and it costs less.

Marking Slides

After you have sorted your slides and separated them into groups, mark each slide with the important information about the piece and write or stamp your name on the back of the mount. This will improve your chances of having the slide returned to you if you send it to a photo lab, a friend, or a competition.

Storing Slides

Each slide-filing system has advantages, and it's a simple matter to decide which method will best suit your purposes. Storage in carousels or projector boxes is great for teachers or lecturers who show the same slides in the same order every time. You keep one set of slides for each lecture that you give regularly. As long as you don't have to look for a particular slide, this is a great system. But, it's not a workable system if you have to pull hundreds of slide slots looking for that one image.

Keeping slides in plastic or metal file boxes is equally inconvenient, unless you're just storing the slides for long periods of time. When packing slides in boxes for long-term storage, slip a packet of silicone crystals into the box to absorb any moisture that could damage the film emulsions. Keeping slides in the same box that the lab sent them back in, coding the box, and then identifying the subject matter on the outside of the box is a workable system for some people. Since you can only fit 36 slides in a film box, you never have more than that many to look through when you're searching for a slide you know is in a particular box.

If you have a lot of slides that you want to be able to go through quickly, a notebook slide page format is about the most convenient file system you can use. After editing a roll of slides, store the ones you want to keep in vinyl slide pages, organized according to subject matter, the date they were shot, their use, or whichever organizational method you prefer.

Each page holds twenty slides that can be scanned quickly on a light table or when held up to a lamp or sunny window. Since it takes the eye only a few seconds to scan twenty images, it's possible for an artist or designer to go through an entire slide collection in a few minutes, whereas it would take hours to do the same using other file systems. Another distinct advantage of this method is that the slides are better protected in the vinyl sheets than they are when left exposed in boxes.

Proof sheets can be filed in a similar way. Each proof sheet is three-hole punched and numbered sequentially (or in code) on the back and inserted in a three-ring binder. Put the negatives in a separate box, envelope, or folder, and mark each set to correspond with the appropriate proof sheet.

To find a particular image, leaf through the binder of proof sheets, find the number of the proof sheet you need, and look up the corresponding set of negatives to locate the exact one you want. If you carefully replace negatives and slides in their proper spaces, you should find this file system entirely workable.

Viewing Slides

The 35mm slide image is a bit small for comfortable unaided viewing; it needs to be projected or enlarged in some way. Unfortunately, the many methods of slide enlargement all have their disadvantages—especially in an interview situation. All an artist or designer can do is choose the least awkward of the methods and design his portfolio presentation around it.

Slide Projectors

Although slides look better projected than viewed any other way, the gymnastics involved in creating an effective presentation in someone else's office usually preclude this method of showing your work. Unless the interviewer comes to your studio, there is rarely adequate setup time and space—let alone a projection screen—in an interview situation. Add to this the nervousness of the typical interviewee and you can see that projecting your slides is best left to less-pressured presentations.

Slide Viewers

Another method of showing your slides is to provide a handheld or desktop viewer that enlarges one hand-inserted slide at a time. The disadvantages of this system are that the slides have to be arranged individually and stacked right-side up, facing the proper direction. A lot of fumbling is usually involved and since the slides are out of their boxes or page protectors, they're difficult to protect from the interviewer's possible carelessness. It's also awkward to operate the viewer, explain the slide, and prepare for the next one simultaneously.

There are more expensive viewers that will accept stacks of slides, which is somewhat more convenient. But there are problems even with these viewers: the interviewer has to be shown how to use the device, and if a slide in the stack is upside down, there's the hassle of trying to flip it. Again, more fumbling.

Slide Pages

In many ways the best solution is to carry your slides in the slide pages discussed previously. With them, carry a loupe and a small, narrow fluorescent light box. Sold in hardware stores as an under-shelf lighting fixture, this lightweight and surprisingly inexpensive light box will allow you to show as many slides as you want.

Before you set out make sure you have enough cord to reach a reasonable distance, then, when you arrive at your interview, just plug the box into a wall socket and give the interviewer your loupe. With a sheet of slides and the light box, he or she will be able to quickly scan up to twenty images very quickly and then, with the loupe, inspect the slides of interest with more attention. This way you get to show the sharp detail and color of your slides. At the same time, the interviewer can read your markings on each slide, making it simple for him or her to check size and material information while viewing the image. And you will be using very little desktop space.

Achieving Accuracy with Slides

35mm slides have become a vital part of art, design, and education. They're a versatile, reasonably inexpensive, and perfectly acceptable means of communication in the visual professions. But they're not perfect. The artist or designer who must rely on them to convey information or to document processes must be aware of the problems that slides pose. First, anything that is large will lose some detail when it's reduced to a 35mm size. Very detailed, elaborate, or delicate artwork, is bound to lose much more than work that's bright, bold, and simple. On pieces where texture is important, it's difficult to accurately capture the tactile qualities that are readily apparent in the original. Subtle changes in color or value are often lost in slides, as are delicate nuances in line and shading. It would be foolish to alter your original work just to make more appealing slides, so all an artist or designer can do is live with the problem and learn to take slides of the highest possible quality that capture as much of the subtlety of the work as possible.

Handling Slides Properly

Even if you take very good care of your slides, someone else who looks at them may not. There are, however, a few methods you can use to help protect them against the negligence of others. Slides and negatives are nothing more than chemical coatings of various colors and thicknesses on strips of acetate. These coatings are very delicate and easily damaged.

Fingerprints on film are permanent; the oil from fingers etches the emulsion of the film and permanently alters the image. A film cleaner may be able to remove the oil residue from a fingerprint, but it can never undo the etching process. Never touch a slide or negative with your bare hands. If you must handle the film, use the cotton gloves sold in photo stores for that purpose.

Dust and dirt can accumulate on slides and reduce their quality. Most can be removed with film cleaner and the proper tissue or by blasting the film with spray from a can of compressed air. All these supplies are carried by camera stores.

Light and heat have permanent effects on slide colors. All slides fade and change with age, but exposure to strong light or heat accelerates the aging process. Therefore, never leave a slide in a projector any longer than necessary.

Consider, too, that if your slides are ever included in a continuous slide presentation— for example, in a museum, display, or gallery exhibit that might run continuously for several hours a day—you would be wise to use duplicate slides and to keep the originals stored or filed safely. The constant light and heat of a programmed slide projector can quickly reduce the quality of your slides.

Color Prints

Color prints are necessary for most portfolios, yet having them made can be frustrating because there are several processes by which they can be printed. Each process has its own set of advantages and disadvantages, and none gives consistently satisfactory results. You'll be able to select the best process for your requirements by knowing more about what's available.

Negative-to-Print

The typical way to have color prints made is to shoot with a color print film: Kodacolor and Vericolor are good standards. From these negatives you can have enlarged color prints made and expect fairly good color representation. The disadvantage of this method is that you must have small prints made before you can tell which images you want blown up to portfolio size.

Your procedure should run something like black-and-white film processing: Shoot the film; send it to a photo lab for processing; ask for a contact sheet from the negatives; go over the contact sheet carefully, selecting the images of which you want large prints; return the negatives to the lab with the contact sheet and instructions; receive your negatives, contact sheet, and enlargements. This is the method commercial photographers use.

Slide-to-Print

With improved photo technology, two other color print processes have become popular, especially among artists and designers who need both slides and color prints in their professions. They are "R" type and Cibachrome processes (see also pages 43–44 above). In both, the print is made directly from a slide transparency instead of from a negative. Therefore, the intermediate step of having a snapshot made from each negative is eliminated. Looking at a roll of slides with a projector or viewer or on a light table, the artist can select the images he or she wants enlarged without having to match snapshots to negatives.

Using either of these processes, your procedure goes something like this: Shoot a roll of slide film (Ektachrome is a good standard); send it in for processing; inspect each of the slides, selecting the best to be enlarged; send the slides back to the lab with your enlarging instructions; receive your slides and enlargements.

The loss of quality in the slide-to-print method can be controlled somewhat by choosing one technique over another. "R" type prints usually have less contrast than Cibachrome prints. R-prints pick up mid-range values well and have an overall soft look to them. Cibachrome colors, on the other hand, tend to be very rich—almost sparkling—given a good original slide. But then too, they can be too contrasty and some detail disappears completely. Cibachrome colors are supposed to be the more permanent of the two.

Another slide-to-print method is the "C" type process. This technique involves making a negative from the slide and then making a print from the negative (see also page 43 above). More complicated and expensive than any of the other methods, this technique's most successful application is in obtaining a reasonably good quality print from a poor quality slide. Negatives are easier to print from and have more latitude in quality control than slides. If you have a good quality slide, however, this method isn't usually necessary.

If you can't decide which approach will give you the results you need, do your own experimenting. Take a single piece of artwork, shoot it with both kinds of film, and send the same slides and negatives to several labs with the same instructions. Compare the results and decide which method and which lab works best for you. Keep in mind that each of the processes will work, given the proper handling. The success of your color prints inevitably comes down to two basic factors: the skill with which you are shooting your pictures, and the care given your work by the color photo lab. If you take the time to run a few tests on these techniques and then select the process and lab that gives you the best results, you won't feel as though you are getting taken. You'll usually find that good quality costs more, and you'll discover that it's worth it.

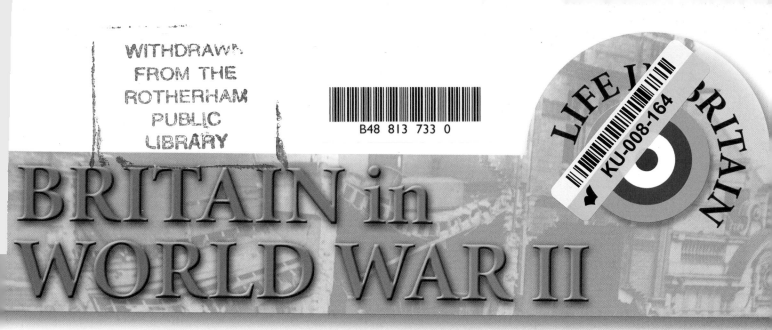

LIFE IN BRITAIN

KU-008-164

BRITAIN in WORLD WAR II

Peter Hepplewhite

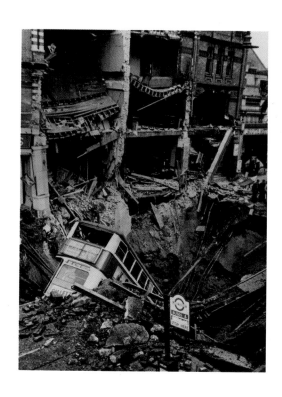

W

FRANKLIN WATTS
LONDON • SYDNEY

This edition 2008

First published in 2003 by Franklin Watts

Copyright © 2003 Franklin Watts

Franklin Watts
338 Euston Road
London NW1 3BH

Franklin Watts Australia
Level 17/207 Kent Street
Sydney, NSW 2000

A CIP catalogue record for this book is available from the British Library

ISBN: 978 0 7496 8097 8

Printed in Malaysia

Franklin Watts is a division of Hachette Children's Books,
an Hachette Livre UK company.

Planning and production by Discovery Books Limited
Editor: Helen Dwyer
Design: Keith Williams
Picture Research: Rachel Tisdale

Photographs:
Cover top left, top right Discovery Picture Library/Alex Ramsay, bottom London
Borough of Wandsworth, Title page London Borough of Wandsworth, 5 top Robert
Opie Collection, 5 bottom Hulton-Deutsch Collection/CORBIS, 6, 8, 9 top, 9 bottom,
10, 13 top & 13 bottom Imperial War Museum, 14 Bettmann/CORBIS, 15 top & 16
Imperial War Museum, 17 top & 17 bottom Robert Opie Collection, 18 Public
Records Office, 19 top Bettmann/CORBIS, 19 bottom, 20 top, 20 bottom, 21, 22, 23
top, 23 bottom & 24 Imperial War Museum, 25 Peter Hepplewhite, 26 Imperial War
Museum, 27 Peter Hepplewhite, 28 Imperial War Museum, 29 top & 29 bottom
Discovery Picture Library/Alex Ramsay

LIFE IN BRITAIN

BRITAIN in WORLD WAR II

Contents

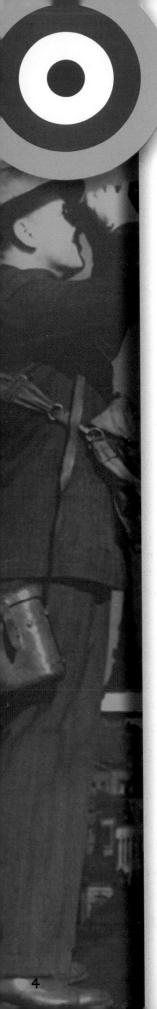

Going to War

In 1933 the German people voted for a leader named Adolf Hitler. Germany had been defeated in World War I (1914-18) and Hitler promised to make his country great again.

Soon Hitler was threatening the rest of Europe. In March 1938 German troops marched into neighbouring Austria and six months later Hitler claimed the Sudetenland, a region in Czechoslovakia where many German people lived. The British Prime Minister, Neville Chamberlain, flew to meet Hitler in Munich and agreed to Hitler's terms, provided that he made no more territorial demands. An uneasy calm lasted until March 1939 when German troops marched into the rest of Czechoslovakia.

▶ Germany took over Austria and Sudetenland before the war. By 1942 Germany and its allies were at the height of their power, controlling most of Europe and North Africa.

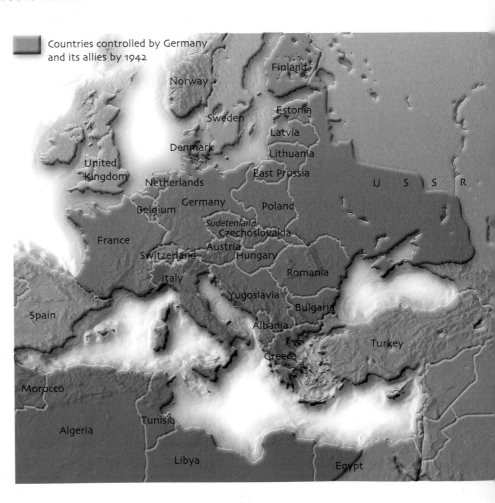

Countries controlled by Germany and its allies by 1942

War is declared

Most British people now realised that Hitler had to be stopped. And they didn't have long to wait. At 11:15 am, on Sunday 3 September 1939, Chamberlain spoke on the radio. Germany had attacked Poland and the British government had declared war. 'It is evil things we are fighting against,' he said 'brute force, bad faith, injustice, **oppression** and persecution.'

Preparing for war

Chamberlain broadcast to a nation on the move. Everywhere families were torn apart as young men joined the **armed forces** and women and children hurriedly left the cities. There was a flood of weddings as couples decided to snatch time together, however short it might be.

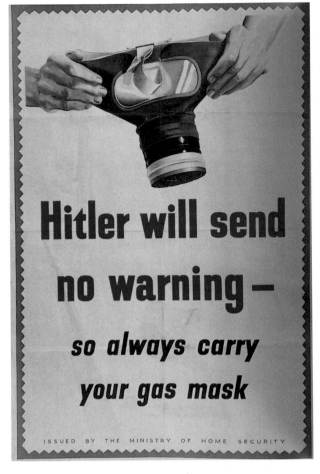

Hitler will send no warning –
so always carry your gas mask

ISSUED BY THE MINISTRY OF HOME SECURITY

▲ Forty million gas masks were issued to protect people from poisonous gas attacks. In the end neither side used this terrible weapon.

▶ Winston Churchill giving his famous V for Victory sign.

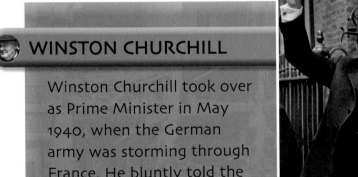

WINSTON CHURCHILL

Winston Churchill took over as Prime Minister in May 1940, when the German army was storming through France. He bluntly told the British people that the war would be long and hard.
'I have nothing to offer you,' he said, 'but blood, toil, tears and sweat. You ask what is our aim? I can answer in one word: Victory.'

World War II was soon called 'the People's War' because winning depended on everyone working hard to supply the armed services. Civilian life in Britain was known as the 'Home Front.' And for the first time, civilians were often in as much danger from air raids as soldiers were in battle.

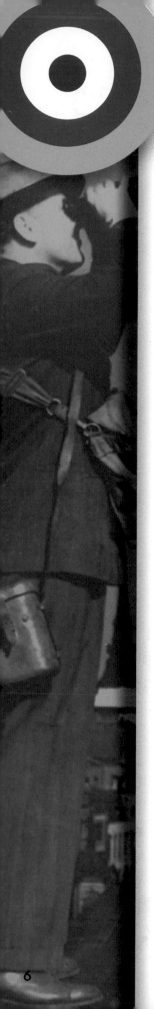

Evacuation

Most people believed that the war would begin with massive attacks by enemy aircraft dropping bombs. To save lives, preparations were made to move millions of mothers, children and disabled people out of the industrial cities into the safety of the countryside.

Plans for the Evacuation Scheme, as it was known, were ready by the summer of 1939 and swung into action on 1 September. In three days 1.5 million people took part in the official evacuation and another 2 million made their own arrangements to stay with friends or relatives. Some 750,000 children were evacuated in school parties led by their teachers. Most travelled by train from the nearest station, carrying **gas masks**, lunches, backpacks of clothes and sometimes a much-loved toy.

▼ A party of young city children is evacuated by train in 1939. The labels they are wearing have their names, school numbers and destinations written on them, in case they are lost on the busy platforms.

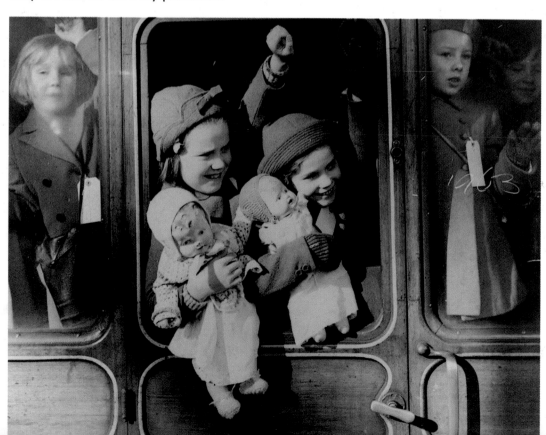

Urban poverty uncovered

When the evacuees arrived in the reception areas, **billeting officers** found them homes with families who had volunteered to be foster parents. But many hosts were in for a shock! Thousands of city children lived in poverty. They were infested with fleas and lice, and their clothes were often in tatters. Some had never seen a bathroom before or slept in clean sheets.

The bombing begins

By Christmas 1939 many evacuees had returned home. German bombers had not attacked yet and parents wanted their children back with them. But this quiet time did not last. In the summer of 1940 a massive German bombing campaign – the Blitz – began and there was a second evacuation with a million mothers and children leaving London and other big cities. The last evacuation came in the summer of 1944 when new bombs – V-1 and V-2 rockets – fell on London and the South East.

EVACUEE TALES

First bath
One little girl on having a bath remarked:
'It's the first time I have been washed all over at once – but it's nice.'
Sunderland Echo, 20 September 1939

Farmhouse cooking
'The cooking was wonderful and I can remember how amazed I was to see apple pies and egg custards that were four or five inches (10-12 cm) deep. Farmhouse cooking of course!'
Betty Goodyear, evacuated from Birmingham to Wales

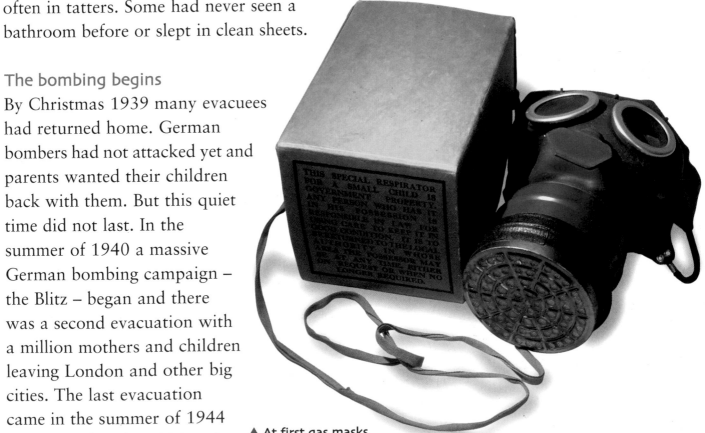

▲ At first gas masks were a great joke with children – they looked a bit like Mickey Mouse, the cartoon character. But it soon became a burden having to carry them everywhere, in case of a sudden gas attack.

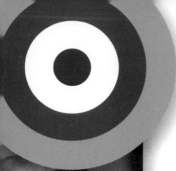

Civil Defence

The British government was very worried about enemy bombers. During the Spanish Civil War (1936-39), deaths and injuries from air raids had been dreadfully high.

Based on this evidence, top experts forecast 25,000 dead in London alone during the first month of a war with Germany – and over a million if the fighting lasted a long time.

Thankfully they were wrong. German bombers could not carry such heavy loads of bombs as the experts had predicted and most of those dropped missed their targets. Even so, 60,000 civilians died in air raids during the war.

Air Raid Precautions

In 1935 every local council had to draw up an **Air Raid Precautions** (ARP) plan. By the end of 1938, 1.5 million adults had volunteered for **civil defence** work. By the time enemy raids began, every street or block had a warden who shepherded people to and from shelters when the sirens sounded. The alert siren was a long piercing wail while the all-clear was a loud warble. When bombs fell, the wardens telephoned reports to local control rooms. ARP Control then directed the fire, ambulance, rescue or first-aid squads to the most urgent incidents.

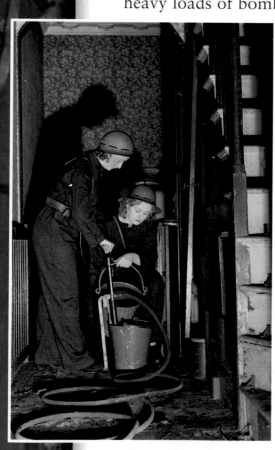

▲Two women fire-fighters operating a hand-powered stirrup pump to spray water on a small fire.

The blackout

Wardens had the very unpopular job of checking the **blackout**. From 1 September 1939 street lights were turned off and anyone showing a light at night was breaking the law.

SHELTERS AT HOME

By September 1939 one and a half million Anderson shelters had been put up in gardens. They came as a kit of 14 corrugated iron sheets that had to be bolted together and covered with soil. Morrison shelters were indoor shelters for homes without gardens. They were strong steel cages 2m long and 1.5m high, and were often used as tables during the day.

One lady in Sunderland was fined £3 – almost a week's wages – when she left a fire burning without drawing the curtains. Although the blackout made it harder for bombers to find their targets, the lack of lighting at night made life more difficult and dangerous for everyone.

▼ Anderson shelters were covered with earth to protect them from bomb blasts. Flowers and even vegetables could be grown on top of them.

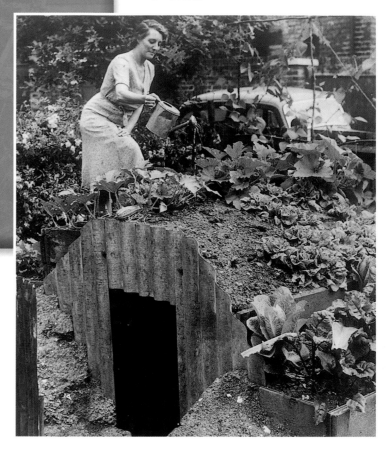

▼ Sleeping in a Morrison shelter. If the house collapsed the people in the shelter might be unharmed, but many were simply buried alive.

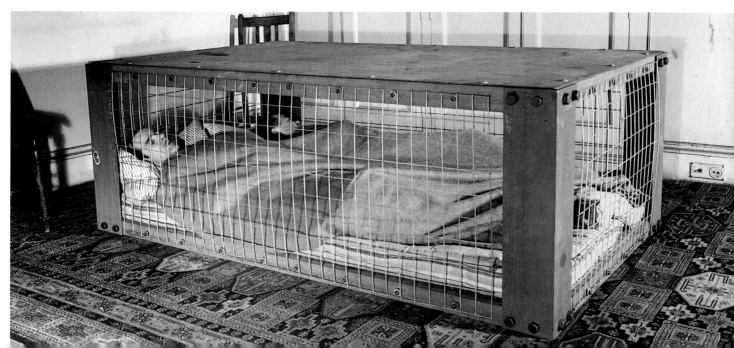

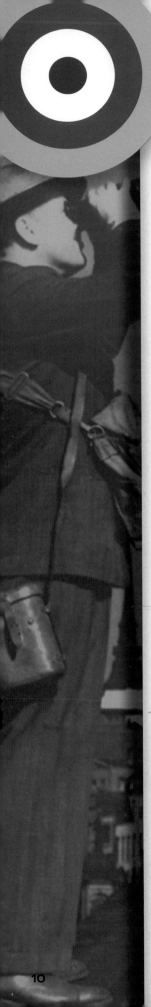

The Home Guard

On Tuesday 14 May 1940 the government made an urgent appeal on the radio to all men aged between 17 and 65. The Germans had attacked Belgium and the Netherlands using soldiers dropped by parachutes.

To protect Britain, a new part-time force was to be set up, the Local Defence Volunteers (LDV), or 'Home Guard' as it was soon known. Within 24 hours a quarter of a million men had volunteered. By the end of July this number had risen to over a million.

Unprepared and ill-equipped

In June the British army was rescued from the beaches of Dunkirk in France, but the soldiers had to leave their equipment behind. The Home Guard found itself in the front line against a German invasion. At first they had few proper weapons. Old rifles from World War I were shared among three or four men, while others made do with shotguns, walking sticks, golf clubs, or knives fastened to broom handles. Uniforms consisted of khaki armbands.

◀ A Home Guard unit with a machine gun mounted in a motorcycle side car. The men are practising fighting in their gas masks.

Old soldiers became officers, and training took place in church halls or parks. No wonder the LDV soon earned the nicknames 'Look, Duck and Vanish' or 'Last Desperate Venture'.

The Home Guard at work

Despite these problems the Home Guard did valuable work. They defended key targets like factories, explosives stores, beaches and sea fronts. At night they patrolled fields in which enemy gliders or paratroops might land. No one expected them to beat well-trained German soldiers. Their job was to slow them down until the army arrived.

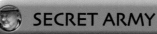

SECRET ARMY

The Home Guard also had a secret section – the Auxiliary Unit. If the Germans invaded and won, this handpicked force was to set up a resistance movement, striking from hidden bases in the countryside. They were specially trained in **guerrilla** fighting – ambushes, hand-to-hand fighting and **sabotage**. They were sworn to secrecy and most never told even their own families they were anything other than ordinary Home Guards.

▼ An aircraft spotter in London, 1940.

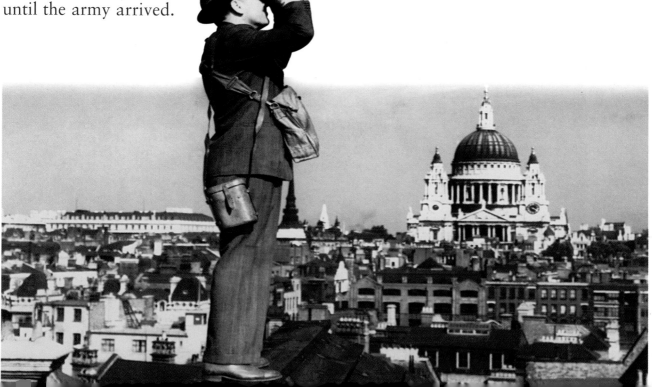

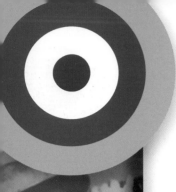

The Blitz

At 4:56 pm on 7 September 1940, the sirens wailed as the German Air Force, the Luftwaffe, launched a massive raid on London. Over 350 bombers flew across the Channel from airfields in France and dropped 300 tonnes of bombs on the docks and streets of the East End of the city.

Warehouses storing paint, rubber, rum, tea and sugar burst into flames. For most men and women in the **Auxiliary Fire Service** it was their first test. The bombers came again that night and 450 Londoners died. It was the start of the Blitz, 11 weeks when London was bombed every day or night, bar one.

▼ The East End of London burns after the first mass German air raid, 7 September 1940.

LONDON'S BURNING

On the first day of the Blitz fire-fighters faced horrific conditions tackling the East End warehouse fires. Hot sugar melted and burned on the water in the docks; rum barrels exploded like bombs; rubber burned with thick black smoke that choked anyone who went too close; thousands of rats fled the burning grain stores.

Bombing spreads to other cities

As autumn drew on the Germans attacked other cities. The worst raid struck Coventry on the night of 14 November 1940. Some 450 bombers dropped 500 tonnes of high explosive and 880 **incendiary** bombs. Thousands of homes, two hospitals and 21 major factories were hit. Most of the town centre, including the ancient cathedral, was destroyed. At least 550 people died and 865 were seriously injured. In the spring of 1941 there were heavy raids in the West Midlands, Merseyside and Clydebank in Glasgow. In Clydebank only 8 houses out of 12,000 were left undamaged and 55,000 people were made homeless.

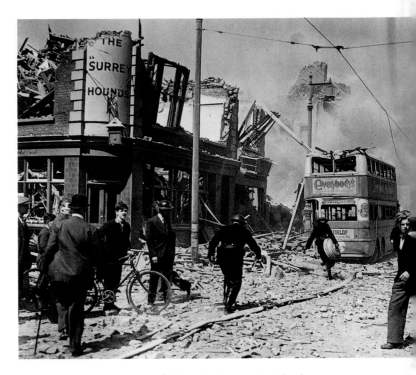

▲ Bomb damage in Clapham, London. The power lines for the electric trolley buses have been cut.

Morale remains high

Hitler hoped the bombing campaign would break British **morale**, but all the deaths and damage only made people more determined to fight on. Even in hard-hit Coventry a local pride soon grew out of the rubble. A visitor at the end of November wrote: 'Having got over the first shock, I think the people are now prepared to stand anything.'

▶ In London the Underground became a vast emergency air raid shelter. On the busiest night in 1940, 177,000 people slept on platforms. Many brought sandwiches, thermos flasks, pillows and blankets. In this photo even the escalators are full.

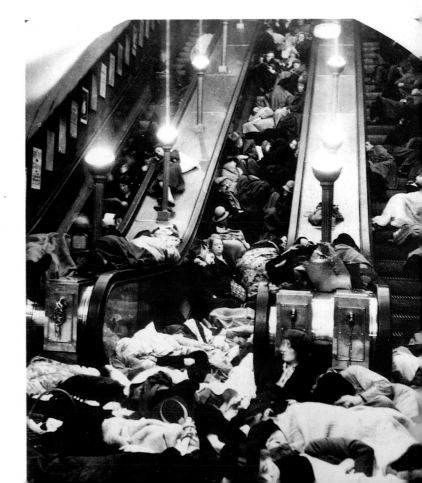

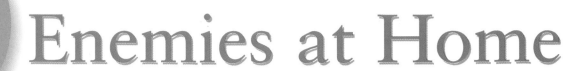

Enemies at Home

In the 1920s and 1930s many people from Europe settled in Britain. Some were migrants looking for a better way of life while others were fleeing persecution. By September 1939 over 60,000 had fled from Germany and Austria, many of them Jews escaping persecution in Germany.

When the war began Britain's behaviour to these new arrivals was often harsh. They were classed as 'enemy aliens' and investigated by local police or intelligence officers in case they were spies, traitors or **saboteurs**.

Spy fever

In the summer of 1940, when invasion seemed likely, Britain was gripped by spy fever. All German men between the ages of 16 and 60 were prime suspects. On 16 May, in an early morning swoop, 2,000 were arrested in London. In June Italy declared war on Britain and Italians were added to the list. Mobs attacked Italian restaurants and many Italian families were put into custody. Victor Tollani, a waiter, had lived in England since he was a boy. When he was marched away by the police he heard a teacher say to his pupils: 'Look at the dirty Germans! Spit at them!' He remembered being upset when the children did as they were told, but even more hurt at being called a German.

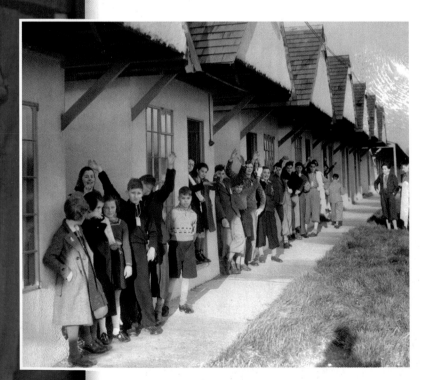

◀ These Jewish refugee children escaped from Germany in 1938 and stayed in a holiday camp in Essex.

BRITISH SUSPECTS

Over 1,600 British citizens were interned too, most of them members of the British Union of **Fascists** (BUF). The BUF was set up and led by Sir Oswald Mosley. The BUF wanted Britain to be an ally of Germany. Members wore a black shirt as their uniform and copied the Nazi raised arm salute. Mosley had been married in Berlin in 1936 and Hitler was a guest at his wedding.

Internment and curfews

Many of those arrested were sent to **internment camps,** even though they hadn't committed any crimes. Several camps were on the Isle of Man, as far as possible from German-occupied Europe. Those aliens left free were subject to a **curfew.** They had to be home by midnight and couldn't go out before 6 am.

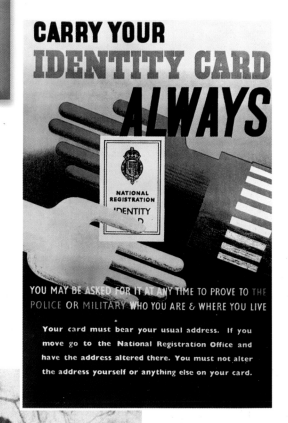

▼Everyone in Britain was issued with an Identity Card and had to carry it with them all the time.

CARRY YOUR IDENTITY CARD ALWAYS

NATIONAL REGISTRATION IDENTITY

YOU MAY BE ASKED FOR IT AT ANY TIME TO PROVE TO THE POLICE OR MILITARY WHO YOU ARE & WHERE YOU LIVE

Your card must bear your usual address. If you move go to the National Registration Office and have the address altered there. You must not alter the address yourself or anything else on your card.

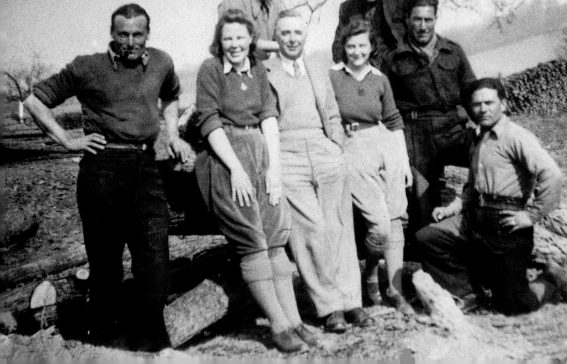

◄Thousands of German and Italian prisoners of war were kept in camps in Britain. From the summer of 1941 many were used as workers on farms, often unguarded. This photo shows a group of British women and Italian prisoners working on a farm in Herefordshire.

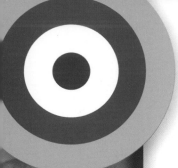

Making Do

In 1939 Britain was one of the greatest trading nations in the world. Merchant ships crossed the seas bringing goods of all kinds, from potatoes to petrol. But by the end of 1940 German submarines called U-boats were sinking so many British merchant ships that the country faced starvation.

Key foods such as flour, meat and sugar were in such short supply that they were **rationed**. Everyone was issued with a ration book that contained coupons. When an item was paid for, the shopkeeper took out the correct number of coupons. This meant that no one could buy more than their fair share. New foods such as dried eggs, SPAM (tins of spiced pork and ham) and even whale meat became common.

Growing more food

The only way to beat the U-boats was for Britain to grow more food. Farmers ploughed up grassland and moors to sow wheat, oats and potatoes. The government's Dig for Victory campaign encouraged people to plant fruit and vegetables instead of flowers in their gardens.

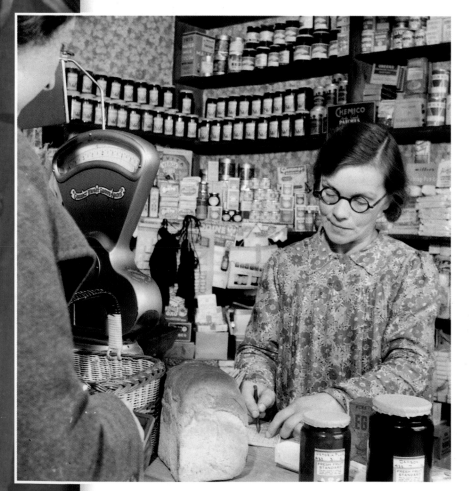

◀ A shopkeeper marks a purchase in a customer's ration book.

Parks, playing fields and roadside verges – even the lawns of Buckingham Palace – were turned into vegetable plots. Families reared pigs, chickens and rabbits in their gardens to slaughter for meat. Recipes for delicacies like carrot jam, cabbage stalk soup and stale bread pudding helped to cut any waste.

Clothes rationed too

Clothes rationing began in June 1941 and soon it became fashionable to be shabbily dressed. Churchill set the tone by appearing in public in overalls. Everyone was allowed 60 clothing coupons a year. A man's coat used up 15 and a pair of shoes 5.

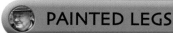

PAINTED LEGS

Sadie MacDougal worked in a **munitions** factory in Newcastle. She remembered: 'For a pair of stockings it was three coupons, so we painted our legs. We got a straight line up the back, like a pair of fully fashioned stockings, only in paint. We used to sweetheart some of the boys from the drawing office who could draw nice and straight.'

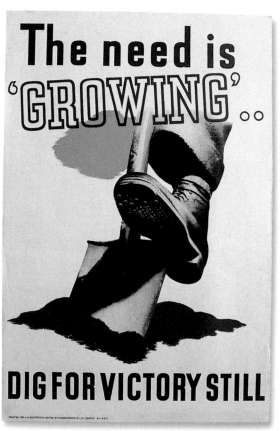

▲This poster called on gardeners to Dig for Victory so that Britain wouldn't starve.

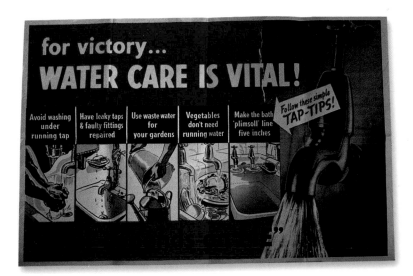

▲People were told that it was their duty to save resources of all kinds, including water, coal, electricity and gas. Some posters claimed that any sort of waste was a help to Hitler!

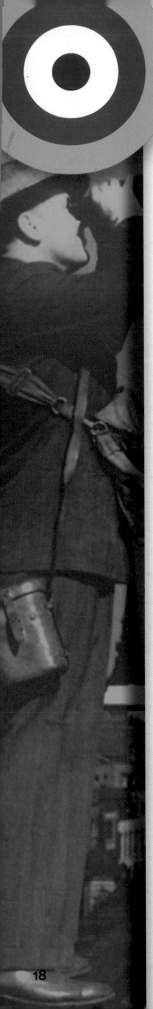

Industry at War

Prime Minister Churchill knew that if Britain was to survive, the armed forces needed an endless supply of munitions. The costs, however, were huge.

In 1943 alone factories turned out 29,800 tanks; 900,000 rifles; 7,000 anti-aircraft guns; 26,000 aircraft; and 100,000 machine guns to arm the troops. Between 1939 and June 1944 British shipyards built over 700 major warships and over 6,000 merchant ships.

Stricter work laws

Ernest Bevin became Minister of Labour in 1940. He was put in charge of making sure every essential industry had enough workers. Under strict new laws, all men and women had to register for work. Bevin had the power to order them to do any job, anywhere in the country. One example was mining. All industries depended on coal for electricity but by 1943 there was a shortage of miners. To meet this demand 21,000 young men were told to go into the mines rather than join the army.

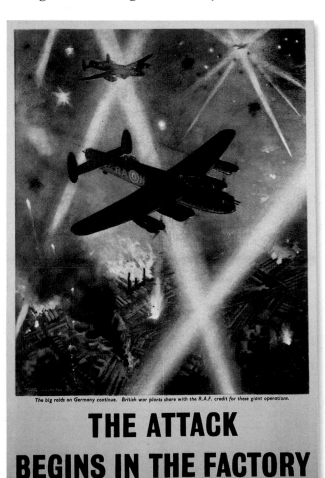

The big raids on Germany continue. British war plants share with the R.A.F. credit for these giant operations.

THE ATTACK BEGINS IN THE FACTORY

◀ Posters like this encouraged workers by showing the importance of the weapons they made for winning the war.

THE WOODEN WONDER

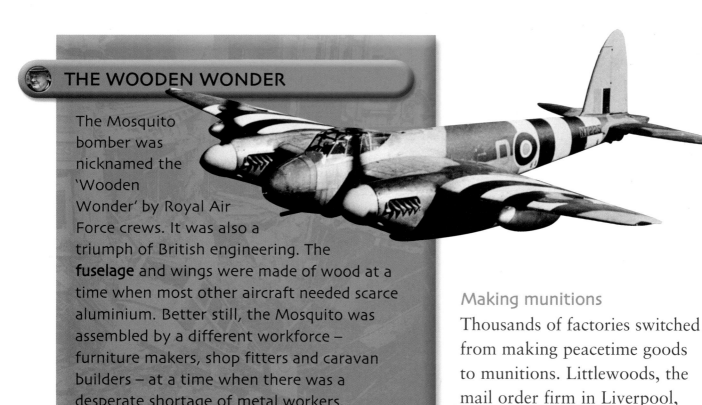

The Mosquito bomber was nicknamed the 'Wooden Wonder' by Royal Air Force crews. It was also a triumph of British engineering. The **fuselage** and wings were made of wood at a time when most other aircraft needed scarce aluminium. Better still, the Mosquito was assembled by a different workforce – furniture makers, shop fitters and caravan builders – at a time when there was a desperate shortage of metal workers. Lightweight and fitted with two Rolls-Royce Merlin engines, the Mosquito could outrun the fastest German fighters.

Making munitions

Thousands of factories switched from making peacetime goods to munitions. Littlewoods, the mail order firm in Liverpool, began to make **barrage balloons**, while the Bryant and May match factory in London produced **fuses** for demolition work. Other factories were specially built, like the giant munitions plant at Chorley near Manchester. This employed 35,000 people.

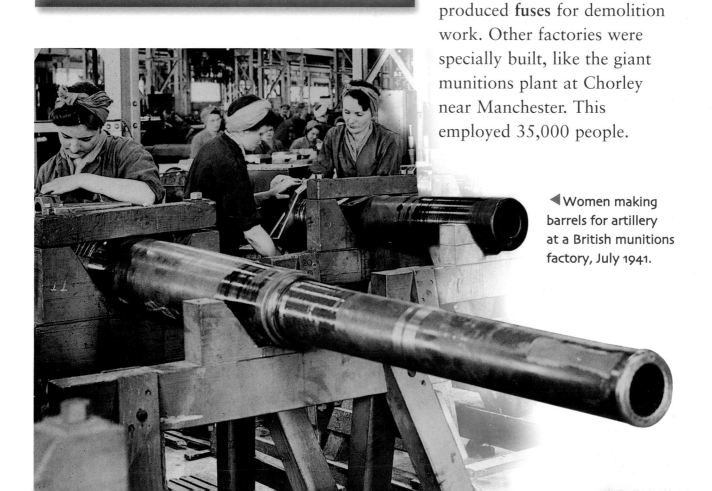

◀ Women making barrels for artillery at a British munitions factory, July 1941.

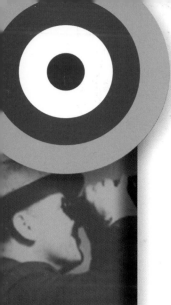

Women at War

One of the great success stories of the war was the vital work done by women. By 1943 all women between the ages of 18 and 51 were liable for war service, if they didn't have children at home. Some went into the armed forces but most took over vital jobs in industry, farming, transport and civil defence.

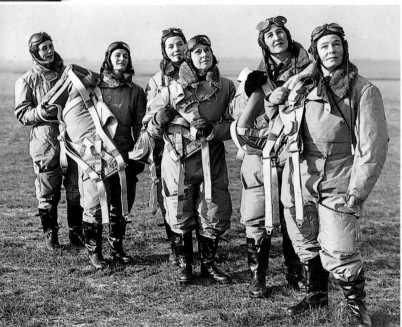

◀Although women were not allowed to fight 450,000 joined the armed forces. Members of the Women's Auxiliary Air Force became mechanics, drivers, radar operators and even pilots delivering planes to squadrons. Women in the army joined the Auxiliary Territorial Service and those in the navy the Women's Royal Naval Service. The women in this photograph were pilots in the Air Transport Auxiliary.

Over 1.5 million extra women went to work in essential industries. These included engineering, chemical production, shipbuilding and steel-making. Often the women tackled jobs that were traditionally men's work, such as welding or operating **machine tools**.

▶Women who couldn't work were encouraged to help the war effort by looking after workers' children.

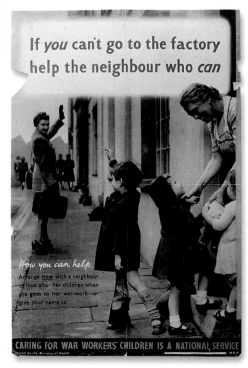

If *you* can't go to the factory help the neighbour who *can*

How you can help
Arrange now with a neighbour to look after her children when she goes to her war-work—or give your name to

CARING FOR WAR WORKERS' CHILDREN IS A NATIONAL SERVICE

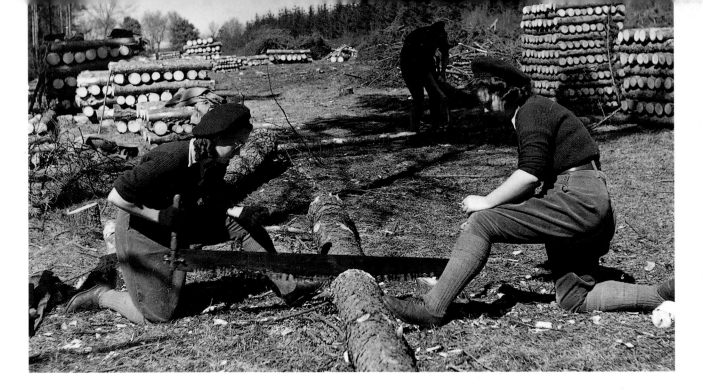

In peacetime Helen Bliss had run a small restaurant, but in 1942 she trained to make aircraft parts in a factory in Croydon, in Surrey. Helen worked 12 hours a day, six days a week – and all night if there was an urgent order.

Hard work and poor pay

Factory conditions were frequently hard, dirty and dangerous. And all too often men saw the women as a threat. In one Birmingham factory the men on night shift objected to their **lathes** being used by the women on day shift and loosened all the nuts on the machines when they went home! Not only was this unsafe, it meant that the women wasted time the next day fixing the lathes.

Few women were paid the same as men, even if their jobs were identical. In the armed forces women were paid a third less than men and given smaller portions of food.

▲ Over 80,000 women became 'Land Girls'. They lived on farms doing everything from planting potatoes and repairing tractors to rat-catching and tree-felling. Their wages were among the lowest in the country. These Land Girls were photographed on a forestry training course in Culford, Suffolk.

 DANGER … AND BOREDOM

Half a million women volunteered for Civil Defence. Theodora Benson was an ARP driver during the Blitz. She recalled: 'There were nights filled with the drama of driving through cratered and blacked-out streets to dig people and parts of people out of bombed buildings. In contrast other nights were spent bored, bickering, joking, grumbling and having fun.'

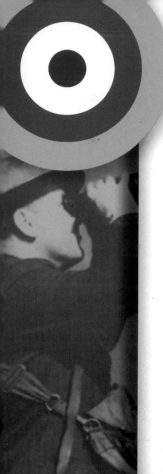

The Yanks

Britain was invaded during the war – by friendly Allies! Tens of thousands of fighting men from all over German-occupied Europe and the British Empire flocked to defend Britain.

They included Poles, Czechs, Free French, Indians, Australians, Canadians and New Zealanders. It was the Americans, however, who made the biggest impact. The United States of America entered the war in December 1941, after the Japanese attacked Pearl Harbor, an American base in the Pacific.

▼ American servicemen in London are given a free Thanksgiving Day turkey dinner. Small gestures like this made lonely or homesick men feel a little better.

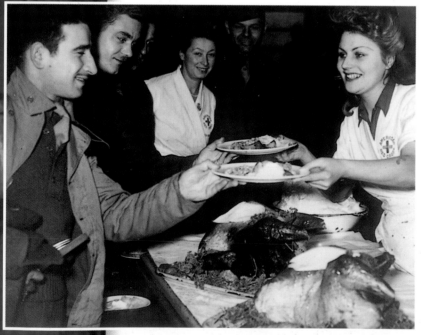

By June 1944 there were over 1,400,000 US soldiers and another 426,000 airmen in the Britain. In a huge construction programme, hundreds of army camps and airbases were built in quiet country areas. A typical airfield needed a concrete runway a mile (1.6 km) long; two smaller back-up runways; 50 kilometres of drains; 500 separate buildings; and a sewerage plant for 2,500 people. So many US troops were based in the county of Wiltshire that by 1944 there was one American for every two British civilians.

The glamorous GIs

The Americans were nicknamed 'Yanks', or 'GIs' because their kit was marked 'Government Issue'. To most war-weary people in Britain, they seemed incredibly glamorous, like Hollywood film stars.

GOT ANY GUM, CHUM?

GIs were always surrounded by children yelling, 'Got any gum, chum?' The fast reply to this was 'Gotta sister, mister?' Always keen to foster good relations, the US Air Force laid on parties for more than 60,000 British children between 1942 and 1944.

▼ American soldiers throw a party for 200 British children in London, November 1942.

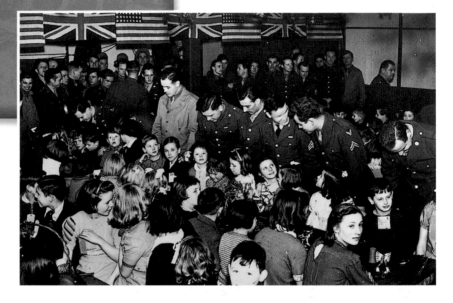

GIs were paid five times as much as British troops and it seemed that the stores on every American base sold an endless supply of luxury goods: fruit, butter, chocolate, ice-cream, nylon stockings, lipstick and scented soap. No wonder the Yanks became popular boyfriends for British women! After the war 34,000 'GI brides' went back to the USA with their new American husbands.

▼ 'GI brides' (British women who had married American servicemen) leaving Southampton at the end of the war to join their husbands in the USA.

Adoption and racism

Many British families took up the offer to become 'foster parents' and 'adopt' a Yank. One aspect of the American forces caused problems however – racism. Black GIs had to live in separate camps and visit British pubs and cinemas on different days from white servicemen.

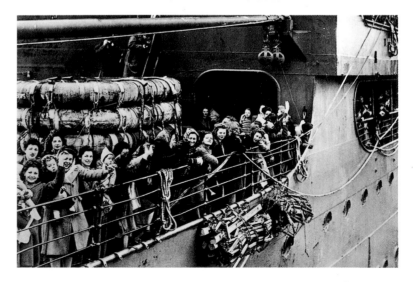

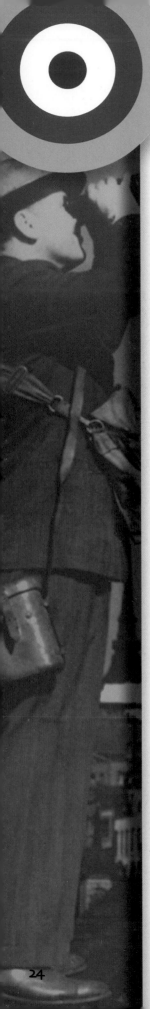

Entertainment

When the war started the government ordered all cinemas, dance halls and places of public entertainment to be closed down. Most of these controls were lifted within a few weeks after a wave of complaints. People needed to relax, and entertainment was vital for morale.

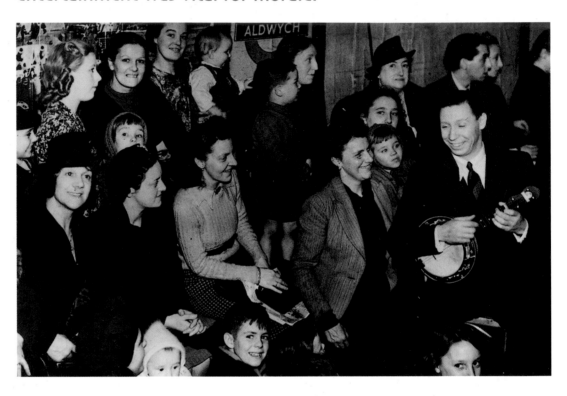

▲ Comedian and singer George Formby entertaining Londoners taking shelter in Aldwych tube station, during the Blitz.

Going to the pictures was a hugely popular pastime. Over 30 million visits were made each week during the Blitz (September 1940-May 1941). Queuing for two hours was not uncommon so customers had to be patient. Cinemas often showed **patriotic** films. Some were set in wartime; others looked to Britain's glorious past. But the most popular movies were from Hollywood: love stories, gangster adventures or musicals that helped audiences forget their hardships for a few hours.

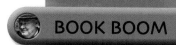

Wartime shows

ENSA, the Entertainments National Service Association, hired stars to give free shows all over the country. Venues included public air raid shelters and aircraft hangars.

Sales of books soared by 50 percent between 1938 and 1944. Due to paper shortages, wartime books were usually slim, no more than 150 pages of thin paper. Many carried the message: 'Leave this book at a Post Office when you have read it so that men and women in the services may enjoy it too.'

In 1940 ENSA presented 200 concerts in factories. By 1944 this had risen to an amazing 2,200. Many shows were broadcast on the radio in a programme called 'Workers' Playtime'. Stars included comedians like Max Miller and George Formby, or popular singers like the Andrews Sisters and Vera Lynn.

Radio entertainment

The blackout and petrol rationing made travelling difficult, so entertainment at home became important. Sales of radio sets boomed and every week around 16 million people tuned into the comedy 'ITMA' (It's That Man Again), starring Tommy Handley. Based in his Office of Twerps in the Ministry of Aggravation, Tommy made fun of the wartime regulations that irritated ordinary people.

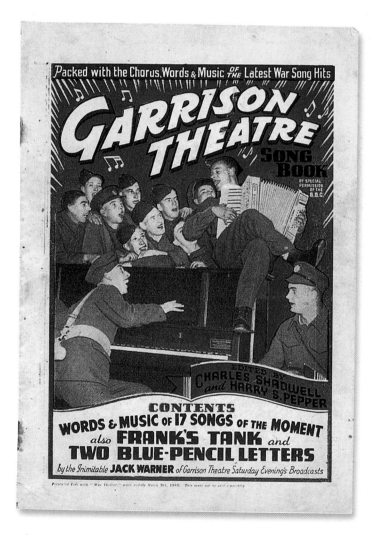

▲ Garrison Theatre was a popular radio programme starring Jack Warner. This song sheet helped people to have a 'sing-along' at home.

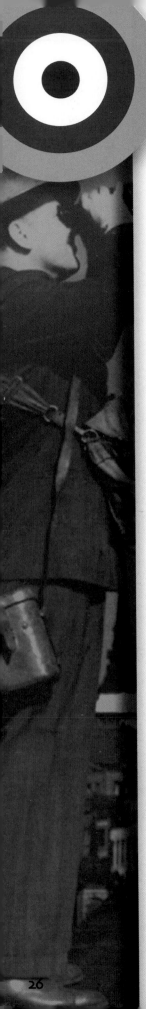

The Will to Win

From the outbreak of war the government used all kinds of advertising to convince the British people that they could win.

The Ministry of Information was in charge of this propaganda and also controlled what newspapers and the radio were allowed to say about the fighting. Across the country billboards were plastered with posters, leaflets were pushed through doors and cinemas showed government information films before the main features.

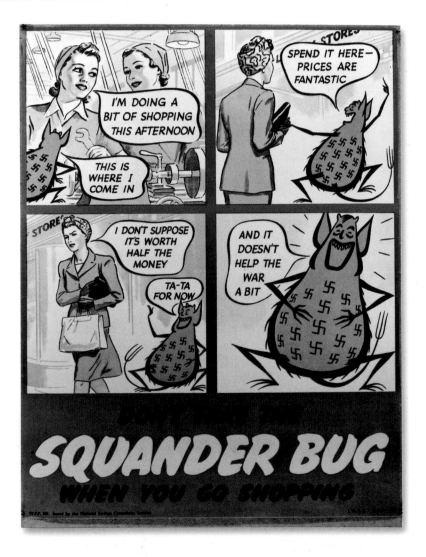

▲ The most effective ideas often used humour. The devilish Squander Bug, stamped with swastikas – symbols of Germany's ruling Nazi party – nagged housewives to waste money.

Churchill's speeches

In the darkest days of 1940 the brilliant speeches of Winston Churchill stoked the fighting spirit of the country. Whenever he spoke on the radio, seven out of ten people listened. After the Germans conquered France in May, he made a rousing declaration: 'We shall defend our island, whatever the cost may be. We shall fight on the beaches, we shall fight on the landing grounds, we shall fight in the fields and in the streets, we shall fight in the hills. We shall never surrender.'

Raising money

One of the longest government campaigns focused on National Savings – convincing people to buy War Savings Certificates so the government could use the money to pay for the war. Special appeals included War Weapons Weeks in 1941; Wings for Victory in 1943; and Salute the Soldier in 1944. Every local community became involved with parades, dances, touring cinema vans and sports tournaments, encouraging people to buy savings certificates.

▶ Tynemouth had a tough savings target for Salute the Soldier Week 1944 – £500,000 – enough to equip an infantry brigade.

LORD HAW HAW

Millions regularly tuned in their radios to listen to the German broadcasts of William Joyce. Joyce was a supporter of Hitler and tried to convince his British audience that they were losing the war. An Irish American, he mimicked a posh English accent with his opening words 'Jairmany calling.' Most listeners made fun of his voice and gave him the nickname 'Lord Haw Haw'. He was hanged for treason in 1946.

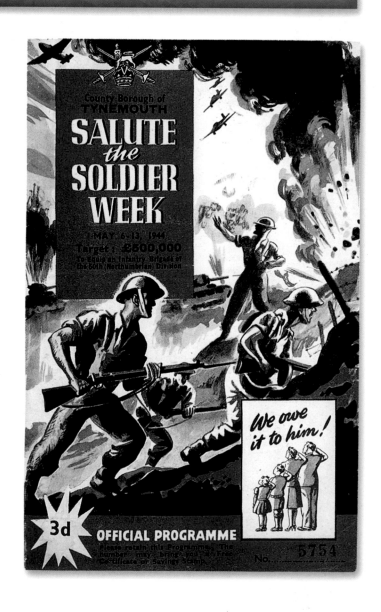

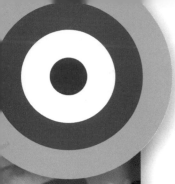

Remembering the War

On 30 April 1945 Adolf Hitler shot himself and a few days later Germany surrendered. Victory in Europe (VE) Day was celebrated on 8 May with parties, parades and fireworks across the country.

One girl remembered: 'Our street had a great big party and everyone painted their houses red, white and blue. My Auntie Al got her piano outside and everyone was dancing and singing. The party went on all night.'

Soon the troops started to come home. Thirty thousand men and women were demobbed (sent home) each week and by December 1945 over a million had left the services. Many men returned to children who only knew 'Dad' from a photograph.

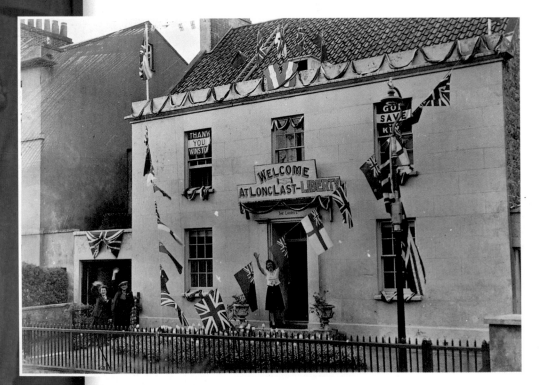

◀ The Channel Islands were the only part of the British Isles occupied by the Germans. When the enemy surrendered the islanders went wild with delight. This house is in Saint Peter Port on Guernsey.

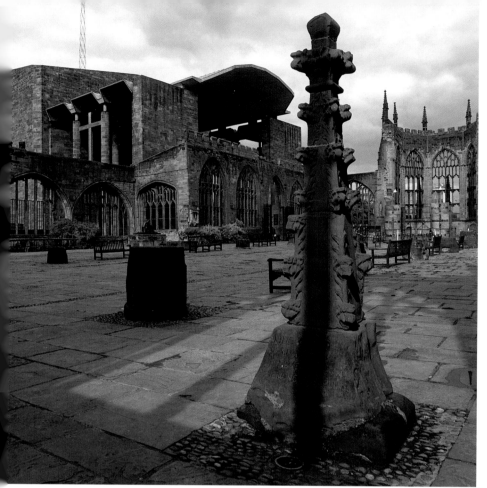

The medieval cathedral in Coventry was destroyed by German bombs in 1940. The new cathedral built after the war has become a symbol of forgiveness and friendship between Britain and Germany.

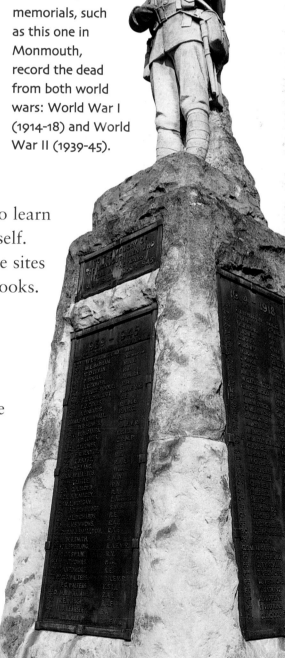

▶ Local war memorials, such as this one in Monmouth, record the dead from both world wars: World War I (1914-18) and World War II (1939-45).

Museums tell the story

Today World War II is history. But one of the best ways to learn about life in those turbulent years is to see them for yourself. All over the country museums have preserved key wartime sites and objects from the time, such as gas masks and ration books.

Local reminders of the war

Closer to home you can visit community war memorials and read the names of those who died. Your local library will probably have photographs of wartime bomb damage and may keep a list of any nearby fortifications. Machine-gun posts and gun emplacements were built of thick concrete and often still survive because they are too difficult to demolish!

Best of all make your own wartime history. Talk to servicemen and civilians who lived through World War II and record their unique story.

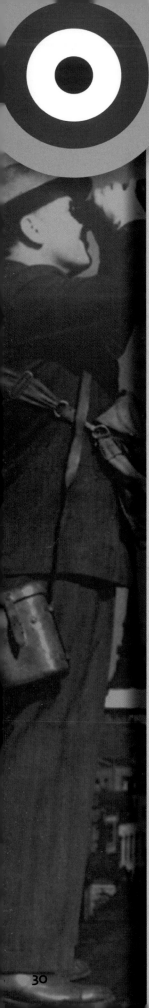

Timeline

1939
September: Blackout introduced and evacuation begins; Britain declares war on Germany.

1940
January: Food rationing begins.

May: Churchill become Prime Minister; Local Defence Volunteers formed.

September: Blitz on London begins.

November: Air raid on Coventry.

1941
March-May: German U-boats sink 142 merchant ships.

June: Clothes rationing begins.

December: America joins the war against Germany, Italy and Japan.

1942
January: First American troops arrive.

1943
May: Women aged 18-45 called up for war work.

December: 21,000 men sent to work in mines.

1944
June: D-Day invasion of Europe from Britain.

June: First German flying bomb attacks on Britain.

December: Home Guard disbanded.

1945
May: Germany surrenders; VE day celebrations.

Places to Visit

390th Bomb Group Memorial Air Museum, Parham Airfield, Parham, Woodbridge, Suffolk
Explore a US Air Force airfield.

Eden Camp, Malton, North Yorkshire
Discover more about everyday life on the Home Front.

German Occupation Museum, Forest, Guernsey, Channel Islands
Discover what it was like to be ruled by the Germans.

HMS *Belfast*, Morgan's Lane, London
Step aboard a World War II cruiser.

Royal Air Force Air Defence Radar Museum, RAF Neatishead, Norwich
Explore a 1942 ground-controlled interception room.

Royal Scots Regimental Museum, The Castle, Edinburgh
Find out what the oldest regiment in the army did during the war.

Stockport Air Raid Shelters, 61 Chestergate, Stockport
Visit original wartime bomb shelters.

The Tank Museum, Bovington, Dorset
Visit the finest collection of World War II tanks in the country, including the awesome German Tiger tank.

Western Approaches, 1 Rumford Street, Liverpool
Find out how the German U-boats (submarines) were beaten.

Imperial War Museum, Lambeth Road, London
Covers all aspects of life in wartime, at home and on the battlefield.

Imperial War Museum, Duxford, Cambridgeshire
A large aviation museum with World War II planes that still fly at air shows.

Cabinet War Rooms, King Charles Street, London
Where Winston Churchill, his ministers and top military personnel met and sheltered during the war. Explore the map room, the cabinet room and the room where Churchill slept.

Portsmouth D-Day Museum, Portsmouth
Experience the sights and sounds of Britain at war with reminiscences of local people, and find out about the D-Day landings of 1944.

Glossary

Air Raid Precautions (ARP) organisation and personnel that protected and rescued people during bomb attacks from the air.

armed forces army, navy and air force.

Auxiliary Fire Service men and women who volunteered to serve as an emergency fire brigade.

barrage balloons gas filled balloons tethered to the ground by steel cables, to cut the wings off low flying enemy bombers.

billeting officers officials in charge of finding accommodation for evacuees.

blackout covering all windows and turning off all lights at night so that no lights showed to enemy aircraft.

civil defence looking after ordinary people during wartime. ARP later became known as Civil Defence.

curfew a time after which people must stay indoors until the next morning.

fascist somebody who believes their country should be run by an all-powerful government or dictator with no opposition.

fuses devices that set off an explosive.

fuselage the body of a plane.

gas mask a mask with a filter to help a person breathe during an attack by poisonous gas.

guerrilla a person who fights using 'hit and run' tactics.

incendiary small bomb that starts a fire when it explodes.

internment camps camps used to lock up people who are suspected of helping the enemy.

lathes turning machines on which metal or wood can be shaped.

machine tools machines that make precise parts for other machines.

morale the way people feel about a war, and whether they think their side can win.

munitions weapons and ammunition.

oppression control by force.

patriotic supporting your country.

ration share out goods in short supply so no-one has more than anyone else.

sabotage damaging equipment or machinery.

saboteur someone who damages equipment or machinery to help the enemy.

Books and Websites

Books

Asa Briggs, *Go To It*, Mitchell Beazley, 2000

Alan Childs, *A Day in the Life of a World War II Evacuee*, Wayland, 2000

Peter Hepplewhite, *My War: Evacuees*, Hodder Wayland, 2003

Peter Hepplewhite, *My War: RAF*, Hodder Wayland, 2003

Rebecca Hunter and Angela Downey, *Grandma's War*, Evans, 1999

Stewart Ross, *On the Trail of World War II in Britain*, Franklin Watts, 1999

Rachel Wright, *World War II: facts, things to make, activities*, Franklin Watts, 2001

Websites

www.iwm.org.uk
This Imperial War Museum site is the gateway to five top museums, including Churchill's top secret Cabinet War Rooms.

www. war-experience.org
The Second World War Experience Centre is a site devoted to the personal memories of war veterans.

www.spartacus.schoolnet.co.uk/2WW.htm
A great World War II encyclopaedia.

www.bbc.co.uk/history/ww2children
Find out what life was like for children during World War II.

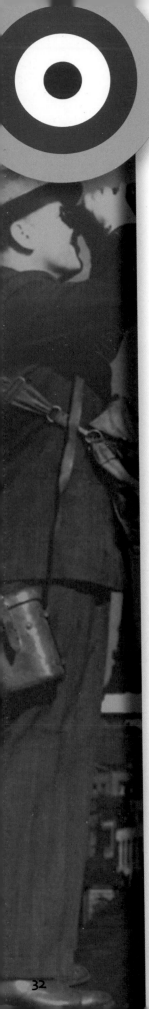

Index